ONCE UPON A Century

100 YEAR HISTORY OF THE 'EX'

J. H. Robinson Publishing Ltd.

Editorial Advisor — John Withrow
Design by Sirje Rosin
Photo Assistance — Mike Filey and Nancy Hurn
                C.N.E. Centennial Committee

J. H. Robinson Publishing Ltd.
1255 Yonge Street, Suite 105,
Toronto, Ontario

Printed and bound in Canada

Contents

Walking on a piece of History

by
Bill Vance

One of the enduring tales of Canadian history is that "we beat the Americans in the war of 1812." It's part of every schoolboy's lore and is often trotted out as a staple when there is talk of U.S. domination of Canada. It makes a pleasant little story but most serious historians now agree that the war, which lasted from 1812 to 1814, was at best a draw. Although our fortunes started well when we repulsed the Americans in skirmishes around the eastern end of Lake Ontario and in the Battle of Queenston Heights, and actually captured Detroit and and Fort Michilimackinac, the defence of Queenston Heights was an expensive one; it resulted in the death of our redoubtable General Isaac Brock. His successor, General Roger Schaeffe was to prove of lesser mettle.

One of the bloodiest episodes of the war was the Battle of York which started just west of the Exhibition grounds and advanced eastward through what is now Exhibition Park to Old Fort York. It was, as Colonel C. P. Stacey, Toronto historian says in his book *The Battle of Little York*, "The most dramatic day in Toronto's history. . . ."

Before getting into detail about the battle it might be interesting to review a little of the historical background leading up to the war. The antagonism was really between the U.S. and Britain. The War of Independence was less than 30 years in the past and bitter memories remained. Young America was flexing her nationhood and deeply resented the Royal Navy's refusal to let her ships into European ports, their searching of American ships on the high seas, and the impressment by the British Navy of American seamen on the pretense that they were British deserters.

The most obvious manifestation of the detested English was British North America lying just across the lakes and the St. Lawrence River. It was seen as an easy conquest; Henry Clay, a prominent U.S. politician opined that "a few companies of Kentucky and Tennessee riflemen could easily conquer all of Canada."

Canada did, indeed, appear a vulnerable target. Its army was comprised of British troops supported by militiamen and Indians. The British were few in number and enthusiasm for the war often burned low among the militiamen, many of whom were farmers resentful of being taken away from such important tasks as seeding and harvesting. During less clement seasons militia service was not so unwelcome, and many probably went, as John Kenneth Galbraith said of rural Ontario boys going to The Great War a century later, because they were tired of doing chores.

Following the Americans' abject failure in four attempted land offensives on Canada in 1812, they set out anew in 1813 to redress sagging prestige by attacking Canadian ports. Secretary of War John Armstrong believed that the key to successful invasion of Canada was to capture Kingston and thereby gain mastery of the vital waterways. Once this was taken it was thought that York and the Niagara Peninsula would be mere mopping up exercises.

The plan was to attack Kingston in the spring of 1813 but Commodore Chauncey who was to lead the U.S. naval attack considered her too heavily fortified. Major-General Dearborn, leader of the American army on this foray, agreed and suggested they take York instead.

There was another reason for choosing York, the capital of Upper Canada. This was the prize that stood in the stocks at the foot of York Street in the form of the partially completed vessel Sir Isaac Brock. When completed she would be heavily armed and adding her to the U.S. fleet would assure mastery of the lakes. The Americans knew what they were after and had ship's carpenters and artificers with them to complete the Brock.

So April 27, 1913 found the U.S. fleet approaching the Scarborough Bluffs (cliffs they were called), beating before a stiff wind. The planned landing was to be at what was left of the Old French Fort Fort Rouillé or Toronto) located in what is now Exhibition Park opposite the foot of the present Dufferin Street. The force of the wind was so strong however, that it carried the landing fleet of small boats farther west to Humber Bay and the troops actually came ashore at or just east of Sunnyside Beach. They started to land at about eight o'clock in the morning.

General Schaeffe, commander of the British forces had been tracking the fleet and correctly predicted their approximate landing spot. The Indians, Missisaugas and Chippawas, and the Glengarry Light Infantry Fencibles were sent off to intercept them. It was probably a mistake to dispatch such a small force because if there was a time when the invaders were vulnerable it would be during the confusion of land-

ing and regrouping. Schaeffe must have realized his error because a short time later he ordered the Grenadier Company to the landing site. To add to his unfortunate judgement the Glengarrys got lost and the Indians were left to defend alone against the landing invaders.

As the Americans came ashore in small landing craft their 12 mother ships stood off-shore and kept up a steady cover of fire. The landing riflemen were under the command of a Major Forsyth while the infantrymen were led by Brigadier-General Zebulon Pike, recently of exploration fame in the U.S. Southwest where Pikes Peak was named after him. He was a courageous and inspiring leader. The Indians' gunfire was keen and although they fought bravely they were soon overcome by superior numbers and the Americans were able to land and gain the high ground. Just as this happened the Grenadiers arrived and the battle degenerated into a bloody bayonet fight which temporarily forced the enemy back to the beach. But again numbers told as more and more troops landed and scattered the defenders.

The Americans secured the beachhead and were all ashore in about two hours. They formed up and moved eastward on their march to York. The Western Battery, located near the site of the Princes' Gate was the next objective.

Our troops were in disordered retreat and the Western Battery was overflowing with the British and Canadians, which led to another disaster: in the confusion of trying to defend the Battery, the magazine

was accidentally ignited. It was an expensive mistake which resulted in the death of perhaps 20 soldiers and injuries to many more. Although some order was restored the Americans were only temporarily delayed in their relentless advance to the Capital of Upper Canada.

General Schaeffe was not at the Battery when the Magazine exploded; in fact he seemed to have an uncanny knack of keeping clear of the action. This was a characteristic some attributed to coolness. Others were not so kind. In any event, the explosion scattered the defending troops and upon seeing the futility of the situation Schaeffe ordered his men to retreat. He didn't go without leaving a surprise, however. Schaeffe knew that his forces couldn't hold the fort so he quietly withdrew them from it while leaving the flag flying to mislead the enemy into thinking that it was occupied. Not wanting the powder to fall into American hands his last act was to order the Grand Magazine blown up. Estimates of its contents vary between 200 and 500 barrels of powder, in either case an awesome charge.

The report was deafening. A huge atomic-like mushroom cloud rose over the lakeshore but the fallout was not radioactive; it was a destructive shower of boulders, logs and other debris. The Americans were taken completely by surprise and suffered many deaths and injuries from the falling objects. General Pike was terribly wounded and was hurriedly taken aboard the Madison where he later died. Chaos and confusion reigned and for the first time the Americans were vulnerable. There was no one to attack them however, as General Schaeffe and his regular soldiers were rapidly retreating along Front Street toward Kingston and the militiamen were heading for home.

But before departing, General Schaeffe had yet another surprise to leave for the enemy; he ordered the Sir Isaac Brock burned so that she wouldn't fall into their hands. It was an important decision and by all odds the best service he performed for Canada that day.

Later in the afternoon the citizens of York watched fearfully as the Americans marched into town. The invaders weren't happy; in fact General Dearborn was in a foul mood. They had lost over 300 men, General Schaeffe and his regular troops had escaped and were safely on their way to Kingston, and all that was left of the ship they came to get were some smoldering ruins.

Recriminations were acrimonious but eventually a capitulation was worked out between general Dearborn and Reverend John Strachan acting for York. Although there was some looting the American soldiers and sailors generally behaved better than expected. In fact they soon tired of the occupation and boarded their ships on May 1st after only five days in York.

They didn't leave without a surprise of their own, however; on the day of their departure they burned our Parliament Buildings, a deed generally attributed to the sailors. As a further insult they took the Mace, symbol of authority in Parliament; it was returned in 1934 as a gesture of goodwill on the occasion of Toronto's centennial. The British avenged the burning by firing the American Capitol and President's house in August 1814.

The Battle of York and the occupation had thus ended and the little town of some 600 souls slowly returned to normal. The war continued for another year before it gradually petered out and Americans and Canadians have lived in harmony since. But as you visit the Exhibition, take a few minutes to reflect on the fact that the ground you are walking on was the scene of a small but important piece of Canadian history.

Cotswolds

The Nurse.

His Excellency's a...

Imported Alderney
Mulberry 1st

Ayrshire — "Burns Jeanne"

Born out of protest

by
John Withrow

The Canadian National Exhibition, while born in political protest, was founded upon a vital need of the community and its times — the encouragement of agriculture, manufactures, industry and commerce.

It is appropriate that the present Exhibition Place includes the site of the earliest local trading post. In 1749, the French erected a fortified trading post on the north side of Lake Ontario, a few miles east of the Humber River which at that time was a navigable river and served as a trading route for Indian canoes. While officially named Fort Rouille, after France's Minister of Marine, it was generally known as Fort Toronto, and was so marked on many maps. A contemporary report said it was "well built piece upon piece, but was useful only for trade". As a trading post, it had some success and attracted many Indians who otherwise would have crossed the lake to trade — and as a fort, it easily repulsed several Indian attacks. In 1759, the Fort was burned by the French to prevent it from falling into the hands of the English. Today, the site of this early trading centre is found in the south-west portion of the grounds, still overlooking the lake, and is marked with a cairn placed there in 1878, and a more imposing monument erected in 1888. A commemorative plaque on the monument tells the story of Fort Rouille — and stands guarded by ancient cannon.

Scenes at the Exhibition 1878.

Upper Canada, under English rule, soon developed as an agricultural colony, for when the forest was cleared, and settlements established, the land was found to be fertile and productive. In 1792, the first agricultural society in Upper Canada, the Niagara Agricultural Society, was founded. Governor John Graves Simcoe, as its first patron, showed his support by donating $40 annually during his administration to be used as premiums to encourage agriculture. Beyond this, there was little encouragement offered to agriculture by the government in ensuing years, until 1801, when the Society for the Encouragement of Arts, Manufactures and Commerce, of London, England, (now the Royal Society of Arts, this venerable society, founded in 1754, is still in very active existence) offered, in delightful, archaic phrasing "to the person who shall sow hemp (in drills at least 18 inches assunder) the greatest quantity of land in the Province of Upper Canada . . . and shall, at the proper season, caused to be plucked the summer hemp — The Gold Medal, or Fifty Guineas". This award, and others soon offered in conjunction with it, fostered a healthy agricultural project in the province, and acreage and cultivation steadily increased until war broke out in 1812 between England and the United States.

In 1820, a "Cattle Show" was held in York (now Toronto) under the auspices of the local Agricultural Society and prizes offered for the different grades exhibited. The success of this, and other locally sponsored farm shows, and a growing recognition of the need of a broader base of agriculture, other than the cultivation of hemp, led the government to grant $400 to an Agricultural Society established for the purpose of importing valuable livestock, grain, seed and useful implements.

This financial incentive stimulated the formation of local agricultural societies and the holding of local Fairs and Cattle Shows — and in August 1846, the "Provincial Agricultural Association and Board of Agriculture for Canada West" was formed as a province-wide organization to bring together, under one organization, the leading agriculturists and manufacturers and to provide a show place for their products.

The first Fair, under the auspices of this Association, was planned for Wednesday, October 21, 1846, in Toronto. The site was to be on College (now University) Avenue, but only a few days before the fair, it was changed to the Government House Grounds, at the corner of King and Graves (now Simcoe) Streets, the cattle show being held in a meadow just north of Upper Canada College, then on the north side of King Street, right opposite Government House. The site was a well-known one — being known as the "four corners of Toronto". On the northwest corner was Upper Canada College, the southwest corner was graced by Government House, the southeast by St. Andrew's Church, and on the fourth, the northeast, a saloon. Hence, the "four cor-

ners" of "Education, Legislation, Salvation and Damnation". It may be significant that St. Andrew's Church is the only one of these buildings still standing.

The Fair was a success, favoured by good weather, and an unexpectedly large attendance, including visitors from many parts of the Province. This response encouraged the sponsors who had launched the Fair wholly without funds, relying upon membership fees and contributions from county societies to provide prize money and operating expenses. A prize list of $1,600 was offered, and it attracted 1,150 entries.

While primarily an agricultural show, it also displayed many manufactured products and decorative crafts. Contemporary reports tell of the high quality of the cattle, horses and sheep exhibited, although one reporter criticized the quality of some breeds of sheep, saying that they had "no claim to the appellation". The exhibit of dairy products received high praise, particularly specimens of Stilton Cheese, and it was lamented that it was not accompanied by "a little Burton Ale". Cloths, tweeds, woollens and flannels, of high quality, were shown, and blankets described as being equal in quality to the finest imports and lower in price.

The display of manufactured goods included engines and other machinery, with particular mention being made of the exhibit of stoves and furnaces as having "attained a greater degree of perfection than is to be found in any branch of manufactures in Canada". Household arts and crafts were represented by many entries: knitted work, lace, ottoman and table covers, including a needlework of "King David playing upon his harp" and "Joseph's Dream, surrounded by sheaves of wheat nodding obeisance". One critic described the face of Joseph as "too feminine", but added "the sheaves were perfectly natural". A display of wax work fruit was noted as being "almost the very perfection of imitation".

The evening saw a public dinner at Government House that was attended by more than 200 people, including some of the most influential men of the Province. Chief Justice Robinson, later to be Sir John Beverley Robinson and a Lieutenant-Governor of the Province, praised the Fair saying that "we have reason to be proud and grateful for the success of the undertaking; and large as the attendance was, it found limits only in want of room", and suggested that future fairs might be held in a different location each year.

That suggestion was apparently adopted, with Hamilton playing host to the second Fair in the following year, with His Excellency Lord Elgin as a featured guest. Over the next several years, the Fair continued to be held in different locations, as

1848 — Cobourg
1849 — Kingston
1850 — Niagara
1851 — Brockville

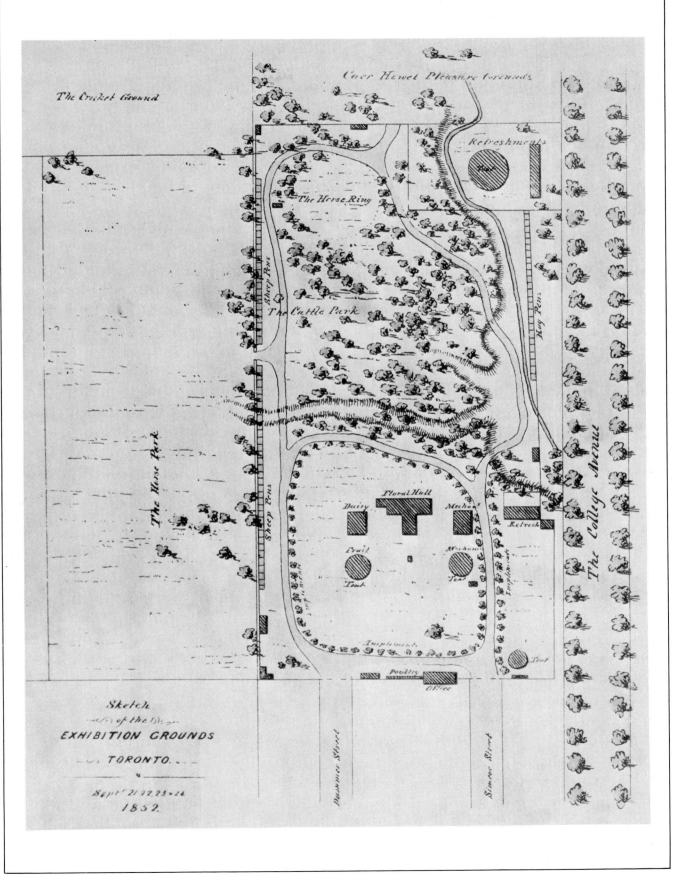

Provincial Fairs 1852.

Provincial Fair 1852

Ontario Government Exhibit

In September 1852, the Fair returned to Toronto, and by now its time had been extended to four days, and the site was on the west side of College (now University) Avenue — approximately between Queen and Dundas Streets of today. The Horse Park on the west side of the grounds was loaned to the Fair by Mrs. Boulton, who lived in the Grange (now part of the Art Gallery of Ontario), and it was bounded on the north by the Caer Howell Pleasure Grounds (possibly a forerunner of the present Midway). Again, the Fair was a success, attracting more than 30,000 visitors. Woodcuts of the period show several tents and three fairly substantial, but temporary, wooden buildings to house the exhibits. The Press found shortcomings in the Fair, particularly in accommodation for the exhibits and the large crowd, saying that "the halls were altogether too small and were not of the best construction to accommodate a crowd. The crowds of people which passed into them on the great public days of the show were always disappointed as they got little more than a glimpse of the various articles exhibited as they were borne along half stifled through the narrow passages."

The exhibitors too were often grievously disappointed, some of them at having their productions disposed beyond the line of vision, others with having their more delicate handiwork destroyed by the rain pouring through the leaking structure". The newspaper suggested that the time was fast coming

when a permanent site should be found, but little came of it, for the Fair continued to travel:

1853 — Hamilton
1854 — London
1855 — Cobourg

In September 1857, the Eleventh Provincial Exhibition was held in Kingston on some twenty acres of land that was part of the Penitentiary Farm Lot and located about a mile outside of the town. This Exhibition featured a large and handsome Crystal Palace, the outer walls of which were formed of thick ribbed glass that had been specially imported from England. It was planned as a permanent building, for future agricultural shows and other purposes, and was in the form of a Greek Cross, each of the transepts being 1900 feet in length and 56 feet in width, and the building was surmounted by a cupola that brought it to a total height of 60 feet. The total cost of erecting the Crystal Palace, temporary buildings, and a high board fence enclosing the grounds — and all other expenses of the Committee — was reported as being £ 3,918 3s. 1d., or approximately $20,000.

Three days of the Exhibition enjoyed good weather — with one day of rain — and while the attendance was large, it did not equal that of prior Exhibitions. The reason, it was felt, was that the Grand Trunk Railroad had not been finished and put into operation as had been expected.

Crystal Palace Building original site north side of King near Shaw (1858-1867)

The Twelfth Exhibition was in Brantford, and in 1858, it returned to Toronto and a new location. Through the efforts of City Council, after lengthy negotiation and compromise, a portion of the federal Garrison Reserve has been set aside for the Exhibitions of the Provincial Agricultural Association of Upper Canada. It was approximately 20 acres in area, and was located immediately south of the Provincial Lunatic Asylum — now the Ontario Hospital, at 999 Queen Street West. The major feature of the Exhibition was Toronto's first permanent exhibition building — the "Palace of Industry". It was a one-story building, built in the form of a cross, 256 feet in length and 96 feet wide, providing approximately 40,000 square feet of exhibit space — and built at a local cost of $24,000. An imposing, glass enclosed structure, it became popularly known as the Crystal Palace.

This Exhibition was opened with impressive ceremony — to an audience of 7,000 crowded into the new building. The Metropolitan Choral Society, composed of 250 vocal and instrumental performers, all of whom received a free admission ticket as their compensation — opened the ceremonies — and the prayer was offered by the Bishop of Toronto, the Rev. Dr. Strachan, followed by the "Hallelujah Chorus" by the Choir. The Exhibition was declared officially open by the Governor, General Sir. E. Walker Head, who made particular reference to the new Exhibition building and its future value to the Association in the promotion of trade and commerce. The ceremony closed with the singing of the 100th Psalm, and the National Anthem.

The four days of the Exhibition, Sept. 28 to Oct. 1, were well attended, attracting record crowds at an admission price of 25 cents — and 5,559 exhibits competed for $11,000 in prizes. The attendance was swelled by the admission — free of charges — of the officers and soldiers of the garrison; providing that the men were in uniform and in charge of a non-commissioned officer, not more than 50 being admitted at one time.

Despite the new building — and the success of the Thirteenth Exhibition, it continued its travels, but lack of accommodation in some of the smaller centres restricted it to four future locations: Toronto, Kingston, Hamilton and London. Kingston played host in 1859, and the following year, Hamilton, when the Prince of Wales, later to be Edward VII, attended, and presented a $1,000 prize fund, the interest on it to be offered annually as the "Prince of Wales Prize".

In 1861 the site was London, and in 1862, it returned to Toronto, and a further 12 acres of land were pressed into service to accommodate the needs of the ever-expanding Exhibition. The Exhibition returned again to Toronto in 1866, it having been realized the year before when it was held in London that the lack of facilities for handling the increasing crowds of visitors hampered the Exhibition, and that more ade-

The Horse Ring, Provincial Exhibition, Toronto

quate accommodation was required and again it was suggested that "the permanent centralization of the Association" would be the only effective solution. This was again ignored, but the Toronto facilities attracted the Exhibition back in 1870, 1874 and 1878.

The year 1878 was to be an important one to Toronto — for not only was it the last one to be held under the auspices of the Provincial Agricultural Association of Upper Canada — but it was to be the direct predecessor of the present Canadian National Exhibition.

The Toronto City Council in 1877 recognized the value of the Exhibition to the city — and the need of more suitable land if it were to find a permanent home in Toronto, and in April 1878, leased the westerly portion of the Garrison Reserve, an area of 51¾ acres, for a term of 20 years, renewable, at a rental of $100 a year, an an exhibition grounds. This land is still part of the present Exhibition Place, but at that time, the lake frontage was only 450 feet. The larger space now available — and the promise of better buildings — helped secure the 1878 Exhibition for Toronto over the counter claims of Guelph and Ottawa — and an Exhibition Committee was formed under the chairmanship of Alderman John J. Withrow.

First, new and larger buildings were required, and $150,000 was budgeted for that purpose, but the local Property Owners' Association opposed this large amount and a by-law to raise the money was defeated when presented to the ratepayers. City Council was still desirous of securing the Exhibition, and placed $75,000 in the estimates, and submitted a further by-law to the ratepayers to provide the extra $75,000, but it was again defeated. Undaunted, the Committee proceeded with the $75,000 available from the Council — and in 90 days, the new Exhibition grounds were ready, hailed as the finest in the country.

The 1878 Exhibition was the most successful yet — with better situated and more commodious grounds, several permanent type buildings, and the Crystal Palace which had been moved from its former loca-

Exhibition grounds 1879

FIRST ANNUAL EXHIBITION

of the

Industrial Exhibition Association of Toronto.

Opening on Monday, September the 1st, and closing on Friday, September the 19th, 1879.

TO THE PUBLIC.

The City of Toronto having, at a very large outlay, secured new exhibition grounds and buildings, second to none in the Dominion, it has been considered desirable that an annual exhibition, for the promotion of Agriculture, Horticulture, Arts and Industries generally, should be established and held therein, on a somewhat larger scale than has heretofore been attempted.

With this object in view an Association has been formed and incorporated as follows: The Mayor of Toronto for the time being; the Chairman of the Executive Committee of the City Council; the Exhibition Committee of the City Council (9 members), and the City Treasurer; the Directors of the Electoral District Society of Toronto (12 members); the York County Council, 2 do. and the Warden; Ontario Society of Artists, 2 representatives; Toronto Mechanics' Institute, 2 do.; Toronto Horticultural Society, 2 do.; Manufacturers' Association, 5 do.; Board of Trade of Toronto, 2 do.; Stock Breeders' Association, 2 do.; Dairymen's Association, Western Ontario, 2 do.; Dairymen's Association, Eastern Ontario, 1 do.; Fruit Growers' Association, 2 do.; Canadian Institute, 2 do.; Lumbermen's Association, 2 do.; the Ontario College of Pharmacy, 2 do.; the Educational Department of Ontario, 2 do.; Millers' Association, 1 do.; Corn Exchange, 1 do.; and the Oil Interests, 1 do.

The high standard to which the exhibitions which have heretofore been held have attained, their advantage to exhibitors, their beneficial influence upon the city and country, and their unquestioned value to the

people as opportunities for the acquisition of practical information, have rendered them well-nigh indispensable to the progress and prosperity of the Dominion. They stimulate enquiry, incite investigation, promote business enterprise, and benefit every material interest of the public generally. Such is the object sought in the formation of this Association and the holding of its first exhibition in September next.

It is believed and expected that agriculturalists, manufacturers, artisans, artists, and all others engaged in industrial pursuits, especially in the Province of Ontario, will serve their own best interests and further the objects of the Association, by making a rather more than usual effort to render this exhibition worthy of themselves, the City of Toronto and this important section of the Dominion.

It has been considered that the limit of a week, even with ample accommodation, is much too short for the collection, arrangement and proper display of the large amount of material which will doubtless be brought to the present exhibition, and to secure anything like a fair representation of the agricultural and manufacturing interests of the country. A number of the largest manufacturers have hitherto refrained from exhibiting their productions at exhibitions on account of the time for holding them being much too short. It has therefore been decided to continue the present exhibition over a period of three weeks, except in the case of dairy products, flowers, fruit and vegetables, the display of which will be confined to the third week, and the exhibition of live stock, poultry and dogs which will take place during the third or last week.

The amount of prizes offered exceeds that ever offered before in the Dominion, at any exhibition of a similar character, and the Board of Directors therefore ask a liberal patronage from the public at large. The Board is in perfect accord with all railway, steamboat and other lines of transportation running to the city, and they feel warranted in saying that excursion schemes over all the routes will be of the most liberal and comprehensive character during the continuance of the exhibition.

While, as will be inferred from the extensive prize list appended, it is intended to make this, the first exhibition of the Association, as broad and comprehensive as it is practicable to render it, there are a few special features which it is intended to make particularly prominent, among which may be mentioned "Processes of Manufacture," "Machinery and Implements in Operation," "Products of the "North-west," and "Mineral Products of the Dominion, etc." Every manufacturer, whatever his specialty, will find it largely to his interest, when at all feasible, to make an exhibition of a part or the whole of the process

employed by him in the ordinary manufacture of his products. In no other manner can he be more certainly arrest the attention of visitors, contribute to the general interest and information of the public, and reap his full share of benefit from the occasion. All exhibitors of machinery and implements which can be operated in the Machinery Hall and Implement building by steam power, are also urged to place them in motion, and, if possible to arrange for their operation at regular work.

The Art Department will be under the management and control of a committee of prominent gentlemen who take a special interest in the culture of Art, and there is every reason to expect that the display in this respect will be of a much higher standard than at past exhibitions.

In conclusion the Board of Directors pledge themselves to use their best exertions, and the resources of the Association to accomplish the desired results, and to make this exhibition the most extensive, instructive and interesting that has ever taken place in Canada.

Copies of the prize list, forms of entry, and any other information desired will be promptly furnished on application, by post or otherwise, to the Secretary, at Toronto.

JNO. J. WITHROW,   JAS. McGEE,   H.J. HILL,
President,   *Manager & Treasurer*   *Secretary.*

TORONTO, June 25th, 1879.

PROGRAMME.

The Exhibition will open at 9 a.m. on Monday the 1st of September, and continue open until two o'clock, p.m., on Friday the 19th of September, closing daily at 6 p.m.

His Excellency the Governor-General will formally open the Exhibition on Wednesday, the 3rd of September, at two o'clock in the afternoon, when an address will be presented to His Excellency by the Association. Her Royal Highness the Princess Louise will also honor the Exhibition with her presence.

The Industrial portion of the Exhibition, including Manufactures, Arts, Implements and Machinery, &c., by no means the least interesting branch, will be on view from the opening to the close. The show of Agricultural and Dairy products, Flowers, Fruits, Vegetables, &c., will

tion to the new grounds — and a second story and a cupola added. The City Council and the Exhibition Committee had acted on the faith that they held in the success of this venture — and with the hope that the Exhibition might be held on these grounds for at least the next two or three years to recoup, in part at least, the large outlay that had been made. The Annual Meeting of the Association did not accept this view and Ottawa was chosen, by a large majority, as the site of the next Exhibition. The Association did, however, express its appreciation to the city and the Exhibition Committee for the excellent accommodation afforded the current Exhibition and to Alderman Withrow who had been the leader and driving force behind the Committee. Alderman Withrow in responding to the vote of thanks assured the Association on behalf of City Council and himself of the high appreciation of the kind feelings which had prompted their expression. He expressed regret, however, at the decision which had been made — and assured members of the Association that under some organization yet to be formed, a great Fair would be held on those very grounds in 1879 and that it would be one that would not be inferior to that which was about to close. It was, to many of his fellow council members, a rash statement, for afterwards he was told that he had spoken very foolishly, and that he could not possibly foresee the difficulties that faced such a venture.

Support was forthcoming, and the Toronto Electoral District Society which had been one of the first to advocate a permanent Exhibition met with the Committee at the City Hall on November 12, 1878, to discuss the establishment of a permanent Exhibition at Toronto. This meeting unanimously approved the project, and with the approval of City Council, a further meeting was planned with representatives of various interested Associations and Boards. The next meeting included representatives from the Toronto Electoral District Society, the Ontario Society of Artists, the Mechanics Institute (now the Toronto Public Library), the Horticultural Society, the Manufacturers' Association and the Poultry Association — and it was agreed that a permanent location was the answer to recent problems — and that Toronto provided the most extensive and suitable facilities, and that it was a central location well served by rail and water transport.

Immediate action was taken, and on March 11, 1879, the Provincial Legislature passed "An Act to Incorporate the Industrial Exhibition Association of Toronto". A Board of Directors was formed representing the several organizations which had supported the formation of a permanent Exhibition, and many well-known Toronto names appeared among its members: Messrs. Withrow, Fleming, Smith, Rennie, McGee, O'Brien, McMaster, Howland, G. Leslie Jr., Booth, Hamilton, Doel, Wilson, Ridout,

MIKE FILEY COLLECTION

BOARD OF DIRECTORS AND OFFICERS OF THE INDUSTRIAL EXHIBITION ASSOCIATION OF TORONTO

17

Hallam, Close, Christie, Barber, Davies and McGregor. At the first meeting of the Board on March 29, 1879, three officers were elected:

President — John J. Withrow
1st Vice President — Captain W. F. McMaster
2nd Vice President — Wm. Rennie

and at the next meeting, H. J. Hill was named as Secretary. A plaque on the west wall of the present Executive Offices commemorates this first Board of Directors.

Ambitious plans were made for the first Exhibition of this new organization. A guarantee fund of $20,000 was provided, and $10,000 was contributed as grants by the City of Toronto, the County Council and the Electoral District Society of Toronto, as well as amounts received from local hotels, steamship and railway lines, and others who would benefit from the influx of visitors to the Exhibition. A prize list of $20,000 was announced, together with numerous medals for different classes of exhibits. A music competition was advertised for military and amateur bands, with a top prize of $150 being awarded for the best military band, and $100 for the leading amateur band. A bagpipe competition was also planned, with three prizes of $30, $20 and $10. Prizes were also offered for a dog and cat show.

An advertising campaign was initiated, $200 being alloted to newspaper advertising, and $25 spent for 5,000 lithographed cards to be distributed by the local merchants, and 50 large Exhibition Bills ordered for posting in Detroit, Toledo, Cleveland, Buffalo and Rochester.

The first Exhibition of the Industrial Exhibition Association was opened on September 3, 1879, for a three week period, the former one week period being considered too short by many would-be exhibitors. The general admission was 25 cents, and visitors were requested to have exact change, for no change was available at the gate. The 25 cent admission charge was to continue until 1949, but the three week exhibition period was changed to two weeks in the following year.

Twenty-three buildings were on the grounds — the major building being the Crystal Palace, or Palace of Industry, which had been a feature of the 1878 Exhibition. Other buildings included a Dairy, an Agricultural Hall, an Horticultural Hall, a Carriage Building, a Hatching House, a Stoves Building, Exhibition Offices, and a Grandstand seating some 5,000 persons, with a refreshment booth underneath. A Restaurant accommodating 300 diners was also provided — and a Machinery Hall. All these early buildings have their modern counterparts today, but none of the early buildings still stands. The Crystal Palace and the Grandstand were destroyed by fire in 1906 — and the Machinery Hall, which was a major attraction of the early Exhibitions, it being the Science building of its time, was later converted into a storage building, and was dismantled only a few years ago.

The Marquis of Lorne

The Governor-General the Marquis of Lorne, and his wife, her Royal Highness the Princess Louise officially opened the Exhibition, and a few days later returned to view the exhibits more thoroughly, and in a more leisurely style, for the buildings were closed to allow the Vice-Regal party to "have an uninterrupted view of the articles exhibited".

An attendance in excess of 100,000 paid admissions, and 8,234 exhibits, spelled success for the new Exhibition, and subsequent years saw its growth from a struggling Fair to its status as the "Show Window of the Nation" — and its place as the world's largest permanent Exhibition.

New attractions were constantly sought by the Exhibition, particularly in the rapidly developing fields of science and industry, as well as the more basic agricultural areas.

In 1882, the Exhibition Grounds became the first fairgrounds in the world to be lighted by electricity. This was a joint effort by the Fuller Electric Light Co., of New York, and the Ball Co., of London, and visitors marvelled at the glare of light — it also meant that the closing hour of the Exhibition was now extended to 10 p.m.

Two years later, another scientific achievement, an electric railway was introduced. It was the first in Canada — and said by some to be the second in the world — and claimed to be the longest in North America. At first, it operated entirely within the grounds, but three years later, it was extended to Strachan Avenue, and then served to bring visitors to the Grounds. It operated until 1891, when a connec-

York Pioneers on the way to erect their log house in the Exhibition Park, Toronto Aug. 22, 1879

Crystal Palace before large cupola added but with new main floor in place 1890.

Crystal Palace and Lighting Tower 1895

tion was made with the city streetrail to permit easier access. The American inventor, Thos. A. Edison conducted some of his early experiments in the development of a commercial electric railway on this pioneer rail-line, and the system of overhead power lines, and the trolley pole, was developed here.

Transportation has always been an important part of the Exhibition, not only from the practical point of getting visitors to the Exhibition grounds — but as featured exhibits.

Ferry boats were a popular means of transport to the Exhibition, but the depth of water at the early wharf was not sufficient for its safe use by larger boats, so in 1890, a larger wharf was built at the foot of Dufferin Street, and it could accommodate larger vessels from many of the lake ports.

The development of the automobile was linked with the early Exhibition, for its value was quickly recognized, and automobile shows quickly became a major attraction. The new automobiles were introduced by the manufacturers in the Fall — and the Exhibition Automobile Show soon became a special feature of both the Exhibition and the automotive

world. The first automobile shows were held in one of the early buildings, but in 1929, a spacious and attractive setting was provided by the new Automotive Building. Aviation was recognized by the early Exhibition, and some of the earliest airplanes, flimsy things of bamboo and silk, were shown on the grounds, and later in the air, in many daring exploits of the pioneer aviators. The present Canadian International Air Show is a direct descendent of these early airshows.

Communications were not overlooked. Early experiments with the telephone were conducted publicly on the Grounds, and some of the earliest phonograph recordings still in existence were recorded there.

Music and the Arts has always been an integral and important part of the Exhibition. The Ontario Society of Artists was one of the founding Associations of the Exhibition, and its representatives arranged for the first Art exhibit to be held in one of the rooms of the Crystal Palace in about 1895. Since then, the Exhibition has encouraged Canadian and international art by the establishment of a permanent collection, and

Crystal Palace 1904

by the display of many other works in a Fine Arts Gallery, which unfortunately has now been destroyed. The permanent collection is now in the safe-keeping of the Art Gallery of Ontario. Photography and the graphic arts were provided with an excellent showcase in the Graphic Arts and Photography Building — but again, that building is now lost, falling victim to a heavy snowfall during World War II. The photography salon is still continued, under the direction of The Toronto Camera Club, and it is the oldest continuous photographic salon in the Americas, and acceptance in it is still a much prized international achievement.

Music has always been part of the Exhibition, and in 1921, a separate Music Day was established, and it has always been one of the most popular of the special days, attracting performers of international reputation. Military bands, from many nations, have been featured, including bands representing famous units of the British and Empire Armed Services, and the United States. The present bandshell, erected in 1936, replaced a more ornate, but much smaller structure, and made it possible for larger bands and choruses to be presented. The largest crowd assembled at the Bandshell was just prior to World War II, when the American baritone Lawrence Tibbett and the Metropolitan Opera soprano, Lilly Pons, were the featured stars.

Popular music was not overlooked, and for a few years, the former Transportation Building was transformed into a dancehall. In 1935, Rudy Vallee and his Connecticut Yankees played to sell-out crowds, and the following year, the very popular network radio program featuring that band was broadcast from the Exhibition on two successive Thursday evenings. The novelty of seeing one of radio's most popular commercial broadcasts, and hearing Rudy Vallee, attracted many thousands who when all seats were sold, gladly settled for standing room only.

In 1922, an Exhibition Chorus of 2,000 voices, under the direction of Dr. Fricker, was formed and they sang in the open air in front of the grandstand — and in later years were a feature of the Coliseum where they attracted large and enthusiastic audiences.

Agriculture

Left hand page Top: Returning from the Horse Ring, after being judged

Bottom: C.N.E. Prize cattle 1905

Right hand Page Top: 1st Prize 1878

Exhibitors of cattle at Canadian Exhibition 1908

Cheese section, Dairy Building

Judging Short-horns on small cattle ring

Livestock Building 1914

Among flowers, Floricultural Building

Tractor demonstration

New Ontario Agricultural cabin 1913

Interior of New Ontario cabin 1913

C.N.E. Grandstand 1913

Grandstand c 1920

Sulky Races c 1913

Elsie the Cow in her boudoir 1957

4 H Club

Bob Hope and Miss C.N.E. 1976

Memories

by
Gordon Sinclair

The first year my mother took me to the Exhibition — 1906 — saw the introduction of peanut butter.

In 1906 my Scottish-Canadian mother took me by the hand, a packet of peanut butter sandwiches in her purse, to see the great show and I've only missed a season or so since, and those because I was in far away places as a story teller.

I'm not sure whether the Coney Island Red Hot or the hamburger came first, about 1909, but the Red Hot, now hot dog, was a nickel, and the hamburger was about the same price. It was smothered in onions and the aroma engulfed the fair ground with its pungent fragrance.

There being little electricity and no Neon or loud-speakers to carry light and sound, the fireworks' display was far more spectacular than it is now. The colorful explosions in the sky had the whole place to themselves as there was no competition.

In my earliest days at the CNE most of the buildings, especially the Livestock buildings and the

Left: Gordon Sinclair at the "New" fountain 1958

Right: Birds Restaurant

Grandstand, were of wood so there were periodic fires and away would go a building or two to be replaced by present fireproof structures.

I remember two grandstands, before the present king-sized stadium, were both burned to the ground.

It's almost impossible to think about the Midway without electric rides, lights or noise-makers. In place of these we had persuasive and tantalizing barkers who used their own voices, without electronic magnification, to tell us about the cigarette fiend, Jo-Jo the Dog-Faced Boy, Stella, the half man half woman, the 600-pound virgin, or the Alligator man from the swamp.

There were Geeks then. A Geek is about as far down the scale of entertainers as it's possible to go.

Barkers used to tell us horrifying stories about these wild men — usually of Borneo — who lived on raw meat and bones, like tigers, and sometimes the poor sod hired as a Geek, was thrown a live chicken, which he tore apart and pretended to devour.

The most pathetic of the sideshow freaks, fronted by huge caricatures painted on canvas, were the pinheads. All female, they went chattering about in Mother Hubbards, doing a dozen appearances a day and existing on whatever crusts were thrown to them. Happily, they were among the first freak acts to be replaced when electric rides moved in.

Birds, a Toronto family, had a big restaurant in a tent with a full course dinner for one dollar, but only

Weight Guesser

Noronic

the few had a dollar. On August days butter melted, customers perspired and waitresses and cooks struggled.

Grandstand shows were mostly sight spectacles and one that inspired me to excitement was "The Relief of Lucknow", where the Black Watch saved the white people of India from swirling dervishes while the air was made blue by blank cartridges, the noisier the better.

Many nostalgic pieces in print, like this one, make great fuss about sampling. The idea being that countless exhibitors loaded customers down with free samples of their products, usually foods, so that the home-going patron of the big show was rich with plunder and loot.

Either I was so small, as to be pushed aside by greedy sample-hunters, or this phase of the Ex was an exaggeration. In the 65 or more exhibitions I attended, I don't remember any largess in the freeload department worthy of mention.

Some things, like weight and age guessers, cotton candy and teaser style balloons or pennants, haven't changed much.

Both radio and TV had their beginnings, as far as Canada was concerned, at the CNE.

Foster Hewitt, Ontario's original broadcaster for CFCA, and Harry (Red) Foster, probably Ontario's first free-lance broadcaster, both had trucks at the Ex bringing in programs from CFCA, at St. Clair and Yonge, across the street from where CFRB now stands.

The CFCA studio was hung in potato bag cotton to deaden sound and had a staff of three or four. It never broadcast at any specific times, but only on whim.

When somebody with a script, or music, was thought worthy of broadcasting on the air, it was put on, But Foster and Red had no advance notice. They each had fans (this being '22) and no more loyal fans have ever existed, not even for Amos'n Andy or newsman Jim Hunter.

Cynics standing around and listening simply didn't believe this music or talk was coming through the air without wires and used to crawl under the vans and poke around with walking sticks to try and find wires. Then in 1938, 14 years before television became an actuality in Canada, an experimental demonstration was done from the Floral Building with sound and picture, flipping to the Automotive Building at the east end of the grounds.

The program, done a year before the war began and thus first in all Canada, was a series of interviews among former boxing champion Jack Dempsey, singer Jessica Dragonette, and myself. All three of us are still around.

Had the war not come at that time TV might have become real by 1940, but instead of that it had to wait, in Canada, until 1952 when the CBC's Byng Whitteker interviewed Lord Louis Mountbatten, who was to open the Fair that year. That was considered a "special". Actual programming didn't begin until about supper time when a bull-headed puppet called Uncle Chichimus made his debut as the first in regular programming.

Uncle Chichimus, who was supposed to be a caricature of Mavor Moore, the first chieftain of CBC-TV, was followed by Dick McDougall, Elaine Grand and Percy Saltzman with a news show.

The Floral Building has one additional memory. When the Canada Steamship Lines vessel, Noronic, burned at her berth in Toronto with a loss of 119 lives, Sept. 1949, the bodies were taken to that same Floral Building and laid out in long rows for identification. Many reporters and photographers clamored to get in to do their gruesome job of writing about those coming to make identification, so police decided to pool the reporters, allowing only one man and one woman to go among the bodies. I drew the male assignment and believe me, that and the previous experience in the Floral Building, with its glass roof, left an indelible impression on my mind.

Another penetrating memory is that clammy time, about 3:00 of a cold and misty morning, when Ernst Vierkoetter, "The Black Shark of Germany", won the first of the big marathon swims and became the first post-war German — post 1914-18 I mean — to be truly accepted as worthy and good.

Vierkoetter stayed in Canada, became a great coach and his children, or anyhow a daughter became a great coach also.

Transportation

by
Bill Vance

Canada has a history linked to rails. While perhaps not a marriage of love, it was certainly one of necessity! The forging of a transcontinental railroad figured prominantly in our politics and history, and is, more than any single factor, the reason Canada is a nation today.

When the railroads were being pushed through, towns vied with each other to attract them, a competition that in historical perspective was to prove correct; municipalities that were on the rail lines usually prospered while those that weren't either moved to the tracks or withered. By the time decent roads came to Ontario, largely due to the unexpected election of the United Farmers of Ontario party in 1919, the centres of trade and commerce had been established on the rail lines and the layout of the countryside was virtually complete. The highways did not attract business away from the railroads. The UFO party was turned out at the next election and slowly slipped into obscurity but it left its legacy in a network of good roads that rescued the Province from its quagmire.

Left Page: Electric Railway 1883

Motor Train at the Exhibition, September 1, 1922

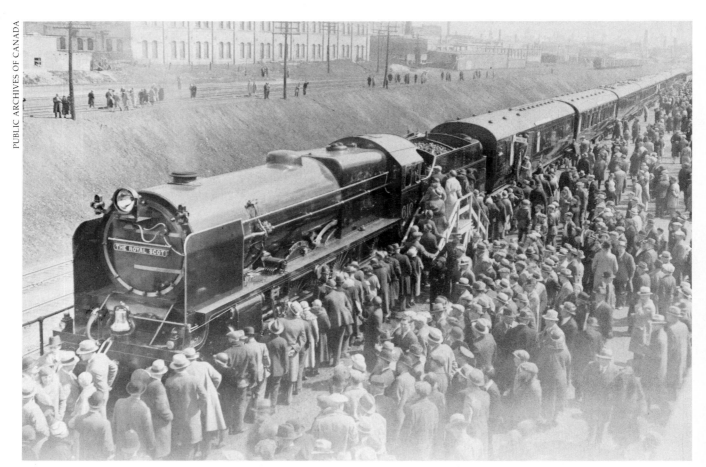

The Royal Scot., May 4, 1933

36

T.T.C. Buses servicing C.N.E., August 22, 1930

Toronto, too, has carried on a romance with the rails. While other North American cities, notably those in the United States, were busily abandoning them in favour of roads and rubber, Toronto wisely opted for streetcars and subways. The fact that she now has what is generally acknowledged as the finest public transit system in North America and among the best in the world, attests to the wisdom of the decision. But the private motorist hasn't been forgotten. Because of the integrated and balanced nature of the transportation system, movement through the city is relatively easy no matter what mode is chosen.

In getting to the Exhibition, rails have played a prominant role both on the transit and the railways. It's no accident that there was a Railways Building erected in Exhibition Park in 1908 (it's now the Music Building, reflecting the declining influence of the railways in modern life). The growth of the CNE from a small country fair to the world's largest annual exhibition is closely linked to developments in transportation which made it possible for citizens who lived farther and farther from Toronto to attend.

The Toronto Transit Commission recognized the importance of the CNE as a national showcase and it is a fact that the TTC carries more than two-thirds of the people who go there each year. It has proudly introduced many of its new vehicles at the EX including the Peter Witt streetcars in 1921 and the PCCs in 1938. Torontonians like their transit system in spite of grumblings and are interested in its new equipment.

It is estimated that 2,000,000 visitors saw the new PCC cars, 40 years ago.

During the first few years of the Toronto Industrial Exhibition as it was then known, and its forerunners, people got (there) any way they could. They came on foot, on bicycles, by saddle horse, stage coach and horse and buggy. But as soon as transit became available it eased the travelling problems of a great many people. Before electrification, Torontonians rode to the fair on the horse-drawn rail cars of the Toronto Street railway.

Toronto was a burgeoning city which grew from 75,000 residents in 1879 to 167,000 in 1890; trackage proceeded apace. Tracks were laid on Frederick and George Streets, on Church Street from King to Bloor, on Winchester, on Parliament and east on Gerrard to the Don River. In 1882 rails were put down on Queen Street from Yonge to Sherbourne and from Parliament to River Street. They were also laid on York and McCaul Streets and the system was starting to look much as it does today.

In the flurry of construction the two year old exhibition was not forgotten. In 1881 the King Street line was extended out to Strachan Avenue and then south to meet the line running into the fairgrounds. This extension was used only during the annual fair.

After the first electric railway in Canada was operated from Strachan Avenue into the Exhibition grounds in 1883, it was gradually accepted that horsepower produced by real horses could be re-

The first Diesel Electric in North America made the run from Montreal to Toronto 1929

placed by the type generated by falling water and carried through wires. Conversion to electrical operation took place in the late 1880s and early 1890s. Louis H. Pursley in his book, Street Railways of Toronto 1861-1921, stated that the local press, notably the Evening Telegram, was violently opposed to electrification on the grounds of safety. It advocated a cable car system instead. Imagine, if the Tely had had its way Toronto might well be the San Francisco of the North!

In his other work, The Toronto Trolley Car Story, Pursley recounts the innumerable improvements and accommodations in service that the TTC has made over the years to help Torontonians go to the fair.

The ultimate in electrified people movers came with the opening of Canada's first subway under Toronto's Yonge Street subway in 1954 and the Bloor-Danforth route in 1966.

The railways played an important part in getting non-Torontonians to the Ex during the latter part of the 1800s and the first half of the twentieth century. And the Ex has participated in the making of railway history; the first diesel powered passenger train operated in North America was run by the CNR from Montreal to the CNE on August 26th, 1929. This was the beginning of the end for the steam locomotive although the "Iron Horse" was to be around for some thirty more years.

E. C. "Ted" Johnson, retired superintendent of passenger service for CPR's eastern region, recently reminisced about some of the special services offered by the railways. "There were Exhibition Specials from many points in Ontario and special 'attraction fares' from across Canada. You could go to the CNE and back from the prairie provinces for a fare-and-a-quarter on a sleeper and a fare-and-a-tenth for a

First PCC streetcars in Canada. 1938, still in use.

Railway Building

Aeroplane Building (old Auto Building)

Tommy Russell part of CCM, the Old International Building then called Automotive Building which became the Spanish Pavillion in 1974

coach seat. It was a three night trip from Alberta.'' Ted also recalled how the railways assisted in the promotion of the CNE. ''They used to send out large wall posters about three feet by six advertising the attractions and we distributed them and put them up at all the stations and ticket offices.'' These broad-sides were often the only way local people learned about the CNE and these ads took on almost a fabled quality in many tiny towns and villages.

The 1940s and early '50s saw the decline of railway passenger travel as the automobile became much more easily obtainable, a trend which accelerated tremendously following World War II. Aircraft were also coming into much wider use. It seemed a little sad because the automobile, bus or plane could not compete with the romance of train travel. Steaming through the crisp coolness of a prairie morning with the hollow, eerie sound of the whistle far off down the track is an experience not soon forgotten. Looking drowsily out of your coach window through a slight smoky haze at sections of golden wheat on a western afternoon is a memory to last a lifetime. The elevators came and went, sentries marking off tiny clusters of population in a land so beautiful in summer, yet so stunningly hostile in winter. Passing through the

muskeg and blackflies of the pre-Cambrian Shield was another story, one hopefully forgotten sooner.

On rare occasions the excitement and anticipation of an Exhibition trip turned into tragedy as happened in the Great Horseshoe Wreck of September 3rd, 1907.

As the CPR Exhibition Special rolled out of Orangeville on the Toronto, Grey and Bruce line on that fall morning the estimated 400 fair-bound pas-sengers were in a festive mood. There was a hint of impatience in the lateness of the train, but this soon dissolved in the euphoria of the adventure. Hitching the three additional cars at Orangeville had taken longer than anticipated and engineer George Hodge was anxious to make up time. Perhaps a little too anxious.

The Niagara Escarpment in its meandering march from the Niagara River to the Bruce Peninsula passes just south of Caledon. The steep incline presented a formidable barrier for engineers laying out the TG&B in the late 1860s. They finally resorted to the expe-dient of a horseshoe curve which doubled back on itself and in so doing achieved the advantage of stretching out the track distance and holding the maximum gradient at two per cent. But this was still steep enough and the radius tight enough that caution was required in negotiating the curve. It was at this fateful curve that the Exhibition Special hauled by engine number 555 was to have its rendezvous with death.

555 came into the curve at what was later estimated at between fifty and sixty miles per hour. The combination of gradient and curve was just too much; the train jumped the track and plowed into the ditch. The engine, tender and six of the seven passenger cars left the track and ended up a smashed and twisted wreckage. Help was summoned and a train quickly dispatched from Orangeville. Amazingly, only seven passengers died; six in the wreck and one later in Toronto's Western Hospital. Well over 100 people were injured.

Engineer Hodge and Conductor Grimes were arrested and charged with criminal negligence. The case was heard during the criminal assizes in Brampton. In their book The Great Horseshoe Wreck, Ralph Beaumont and James Filby recount the testimony of one witness, a Mr. MacMurchy, who happened to be repairing a culvert near the scene at the time of the crash. On the steepness of the gradient he said "The grade is very steep. Two per cent, 2 feet in 100, 26 feet in a mile." One hopes in the interest of justice that Mr. MacMurchy's testimony was more accurate than his arithmetic.

Hodge and Grimes were found innocent of the charge even though investigations indicated that the cause of the wreck was excessive speed or, in railway jargon, fast running. The horseshoe curve was finally removed in 1933 but memories of the tragedy still linger in the Credit Valley.

The inauguration of the Government of Ontario commuter train service in 1967 added a new dimension to Exhibition rail service. Extra trains operate during the Ex and it has been a success story, ridership having risen from 66 thousand CNE-bound passengers in 1967 to 662 thousand in 1974. Nineteen seventy four was a watershed when, due to a TTC strike, GO passenger volume almost doubled over 1972 (GO has its labour relations problems too; the CNR which operates GO for the government was struck in 1973). By 1977 GO travel surpassed 1974, rising to 683 thousand riders. So while CNE attendance rose from 3 to 3.5 million, those that came by GO train increased more than ten times. You can bet that most of those riders formerly came by automobile. The rails are making a comeback!

Nineteen seventy eight will see another innovation for GO service with the introduction of the new Bi-Level cars which can carry 75 per cent more riders than the standard coach.

When you visit the Ex possibly you will ride there on rails. Chances are also good that you won't realize the important part that rail transportation has played in the growth of the CNE during its first century.

Automotive Building 1929

Canada's first subway opened March 1954

Buildings
and
Gates

Lighting Tower on left. Introduction of Electric Lights 1882

Present day Firehall built 1914, horses were used until 1931

Old Press Building foreground, Manufacturer's Building situated directly behind (1906)

Manufacturers Building Exhibit 1910

Machinery Hall 1916

Manufacturers Building 1913

Manufacturers Building 1913

Government Building built in 1912 now A/C and Hobbies.

Ontario Government Building Opening attended by T. Russel, T. Bradshaw and H. Ferguson Premier of Ontario 1926

South view of Colliseum, the largest building under one roof in world when built in 1922

Electrical Building erected 1928

South Side Automotive Building built 1929

Interior of Automotive Building 1929

Railways Building Built 1908 now Music Building

Graphic Arts Building, now site of Q.E. Building

Better Living Building built in 1962

East entrance to Toronto Industrial Exhibition grounds 1901

Dufferin entrance 1903

Dufferin Gate 1911

Dufferin Gate 1920's

Prince Wales at C.N.E. 1927

Sam Harris, Prince George and Prince Edward at opening of the Princes' Gates 1927

*Alf Champman designer of Princes' Gates, Ontario Building and
Electrical Building*

Dominion Gate, west end of grounds near present ballpark

Princes' Gates 1930

A favourite rendezvous – the Gooderham Fountain built in 1911

In 1978 it's still "Meet me at the Fountain". The Princess Margaret Fountain dedicated by Princess Margaret in 1958.

C.N.E. flagpole erected in 1977 replaced the old flagpole of 1930. The new flagpole is an 184-foot Douglas' Fir believed to be the tallest wooden flagpole in the world. It was dedicated August 18, 1977 by the Lieutenant Governor Pauline M. McGibbon

Grandstand Shows

by
Nancy Erb Kee

"This year's fair is an outstanding example of the graphic manner in which the Canadian National Exhibition tells to the world the unique story of Canada's Industry, Thrift and Prosperity." (The Globe, 1922)

Remember? The historical pageants of the C.N.E. Grandstand shows, with their brilliant colour, martial bands and unforgettable fireworks; these were the most thrilling aspects of the biggest fall fair in our nation. Even today's generation maintains there is nothing like the Grandstand shows. Where else in North America can you see your favourite rock group perform live to the vibrating response of 22,000 souls — at such a reasonable price? For nearly a hundred years the Grandstand shows have been a major drawing card for one of Canada's oldest institutions, the Canadian National Exhibition.

The first 5,000 seat grandstand opened at the "EX" in 1880, and crowds flocked to the site, eager to witness the "magnificent pyrotechnical display." Athletic feats in both track and field made the Caledonian Games and the bicycle races great support attractions for the fireworks.

Each year the 25 cent admission to the grounds allowed the chance to see an ever increasing repertoire of special features. A Hungarian gypsy band, boomerang throwers, a "Marvellous" troupe of Toozoonin Arabs and the Stereoptican Views (projected images of some 20 feet in diameter) shown by Prof. Dix — "an image tour around the world" — were just a few of the more exotic headline attractions.

The future of the Grandstand shows suddenly brightened in 1882, when electric lights were installed throughout the Exhibition. Lighting led the way to the presentation of the amazing Historical Pageants.

Some of the stars that have entertained at the C.N.E.

The first of these appeared in 1884 with the luminous "Bombardment of Alexandria."

The entire Grandstand performance was lit by 100 electric lights from a tower 150 feet high. As the audience waited for their pageant they were entertained by athletes and acrobats, including the troupe of Royal Russian Athletes, Mlle Alphonsine and her trained pigeons and the unusual Onzali, who flew through the air with two balloons clutched under his arms. But their astonishing performances paled at the sight of "The Bombardment of Alexandria", complete with blazing fireworks.

So popular was the "Spectacular" that the President of the C.N.E., John J. Withrow, and General Manager, H.J. Hill, presented "The Siege of Pekin" in 1887. Its success was followed by "The Siege of Sebastapol" in 1888, "The Burning of Moscow" in 1889, and "The Last Days of Pompeii" in 1890.

An illustrated programme of attractions for the C.N.E. in 1891, highlighted the "Siege of Paris" or the "Days of the Commune." The show would include "200 people, gorgeously costumed, Parisian Fetes, exciting events — Battle Scenes — and many new novelties with Colossal Paintings, and Pyrotechnical effects. The Production of this piece will entail an enormous outlay and can be seen at no other exhibition in Canada."

These explosive pageants were conducted under the supervision of Messers. James Pain and Sons, the Chief Pyrotechnicists to England's Royal Naval Squadron.

But even fireworks should be open to competition, or so claimed Canada's Prof. William T. Hand. He "flew through the air with the greatest of ease" in a chariot pulled by Fiery Dragons and then descended (with celerity, according to one reporter) in front of the Exhibition's main building — proof that his company was equally capable of producing startling effects. From then on, the C.N.E. Grandstand shows were entirely produced and funded by the W.T. Hand Company. Naturally, each show included impressive displays of fireworks as buildings, ships and volcanoes erupted according to the dictates of the script.

S.R. George Penson, a skillful artist of his day, became associated with the Hand Company in 1892. His beautifully crafted water colours and sketches became the set designs for the "Siege of Algiers" in 1894. Thereafter, he designed and coördinated all the Historical Pageants until his retirement with "Montezuma" in 1933.

The original grandstand was torn down in 1894 to make way for a larger one, 700 feet long with a seating capacity of 12,000. In the following year spectators of the new Grandstand show were amazed to see ponds of water, islands, bridges and boats where the old trapeze poles and nets had always been. What could it mean?

At 7:00 p.m. the performance began with a fancy drill called the Victoria Cross, executed by the Royal Canadian Dragoons. Then came the aquatic part of the programme. The audience gaped at Monster Frogs, Alligators, and lithe Mermaids and applauded the daring feats of high diving. Around 9:00 p.m. the scenery of the stages was hustled out of sight and the white walls, flat roofs and domes of the ill-fated Lucknow were revealed. As the tragic "Siege of Lucknow" unfolded, spectators found themselves drawn into this ghastly battle, fought in India. To quote one report, "The Spectacle was faithfully carried out and the cheers, which greeted each event in the presentation, showed how strongly it stirred the vast mass of spectators."

The C.N.E. has never been a stranger to criticism.

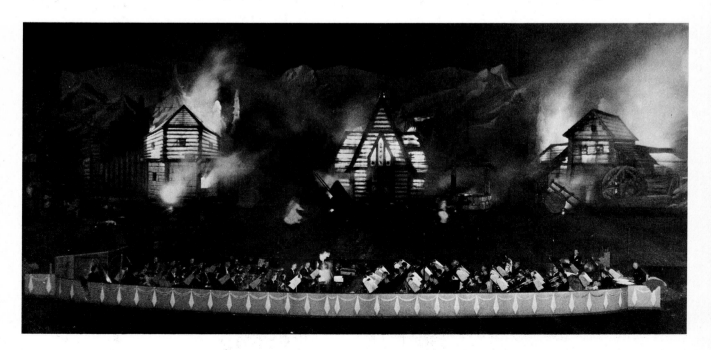

S. R. George Penson retired in glory with the production of "Montezuma"

By 1900, the Toronto Star was opening its columns to some pretty strong comments from its readers on how the "EX" could be improved. Exhibitors added their voice to the cry. Far too much emphasis was being given to the midway, they claimed, and not enough to the products they displayed. In spite of the attack, the Star was moved to admit, "Looking back over a number of years we find a great feature of the "EX" is undoubtedly the Spectaculars presented in front of the Grandstand."

That same year some prominent Theatrical men expressed their surprise at the excellence of the Grandstand show. They claimed it was the hardest time of year to get attractions because the agents preferred theatrical bookings and the performers themselves preferred a three week engagement to a two week. Besides, the new "Vaudeville Trust" law had driven the best North American performers to England and the Continent. Therefore, they concluded, the Exhibition Association must have a splendid reputation to get the attractions it was presenting.

Open air work was — and continues to be — a novel challenge to some performers. Sun and wind had bad effects on certain acts. Due to high winds, the celebrated Holloway Trio had to cancel their wire-walking and balancing act a number of times. Nevertheless, the Marvellous Marsh was able to thrill his spectators by diving from a wheel, high atop an airy trestlework, and plunging 229 feet to the pond below.

Circus and hippodrome acts in front of the Grandstand involved the use of four stages. These provided

High wire act

a score of acts and a flow of continuous vaudeville action that managed to keep the audience alert for fully two and a half hours. One year Mlle Ce'Dora made the crowd gasp as she sped her motorcycle round and round the interior of a huge revolving globe.

Then there were the novelty skating acts and, year after year, the crowds waited for the sight of the Royal Canadian Dragoons performing their un-endingly popular Musical Ride. In 1913, the Dragoons were finally permitted to execute their first Charge (the move in which the whole troupe of mounted soldiers charges the full length of the Grandstand with their lances advanced to pierce the enemy) — but not before the men and horses were insured against damage or accident by a prudent C.N.E. management.

During the early 1900's, all the costumes for the historical pageants were supplied by a John Henderson, "Author, Producer and Manager." He headed a "Company of Established Players" in London, England. He seemed well acquainted with Canada as the company's repertoire of plays included "Under the Maple Leaf," "In Far-Away Calgary" (Very Intense), and "Sergeant Ferguson R.N.W.P.," (Powerful).

The actual presentation of the "Burning of Rome, Nero" must have been an awesome sight. Penson's set faithfully reproduced the several hills on which the Eternal City was built, while the temples of Jupiter and Vesta were prominent in the foreground. A market scene of rich and ever-changing colour had a mixture of Greeks, Nubians, Egyptians, Persians and Turks mingling with the Roman citizens. Nero appeared and was greeted with shouts of derision. He angrily ordered the persecution of two Christians, whereupon Paul of Tarsus was seen in the mob. He denounced Nero. At once a sheet of fire arose behind the temple of Jupiter.

It was reported that the Hand Company had never before attempted anything in the way of such illumination. Previously they had relied on martial glamour — cannon volleys and rounds of shot — to heighten their effects.

This time the pyrotechnical contractors performed solely on their own. Not only did "The Burning of Rome" recall ancient history, but it incorporated some original and modern features. A fight between an airship and a coastal defence fort was somehow worked into a collision between a fire engine and an automobile, both displaying a clever mechanical adaptation of the use of fireworks.

Edward, Prince of Wales, attended the C.N.E. in 1919, just after the end of the First World War. The Grandstand pageant that year was "empire Triumphant," the Jubilee Spectacle. The catalogue gave a full description of the events, beginning with an Indian Pow-wow performed by a girls' ballet group. The Canadian Brigades entered the stadium from each gate with the massed bands playing "The Maple

JAMES COLLECTION — CITY OF TORONTO ARCHIVES

The crowds gasped as the towers swayed back and forth

C.N.E. Grandstand trick cyclists 1920

According to the catalogue, "the Jubilee Spectacle ... presented by 1200 performers on the same magnificent scale as its Quebec, citadel-crowned setting, is a pulse-quickening, patriotic masterpiece, compelling in its grandeur and vibrant with infectious faith in Canada!"

Crowds at the Grandstand were treated to a Military Tattoo, portraying Canada's Warriors from the Plains of Abraham to the Passendaele and Cambria of World War I. There was also Highland dancing performed by a flock of "winsome lassies" from the Somers School. Another group dressed as "jolly tars" won an equally warm reception.

One of the spine-tingling events of that Grandstand show was the dare-devil Auto Polo. It preceded the Tattoo and supplied the audience with thrills galore. One car completely over-turned three times, but each time its driver managed to jump clear. The favourite method of driving an opponent off his clear path to score a goal was to ram his car from behind until both cars were right out of action. The intrepid empire dodged around, between and frequently in the path of the roaring cars. If anything, he took more chances than the auto-poloists themselves. Between the roaring, the crashes and the danger, spectators hardly knew where to look in their excitement.

The Spectacular that year was the "Durbar of His Royal Highness, the Prince of Wales in India." It was presented brilliantly and greeted as the best performance in ten years. With its regiments of gaudily apparelled soldiers, the bright Eastern dress, the elephants and last of all — the Smiling Prince — it drew roars of approval from the crowd.

Leaf" and "the Flag to Fight For," thus heralding the "Birth of Canada." Next came the "March of the Provinces" as the stage set of Quebec, with its citadel-crowned rock on the St. Lawrence, was illuminated. Invisible, a choir sang an anthem while troops attended church services before going overseas. Their ship arrived as massed bands played "Pack Up Your Troubles in Your Old Kit Bag." The whole spectacle concluded with a rousing version of "Rule Britannia" and the Jubilee fireworks.

Dance of the squaws from "Over here" 1921

Construction of the grandstand for the 1948 season

In spite of the depressing economic scene in Canada during the thirties, the Canadian National Exhibition continued to flourish. Large crowds, eager for diversion, still managed to find the 25 cents for admission and were rewarded by the sight of new exhibits, old favourites and the ever-popular Grandstand shows. The Spectaculars were as lavish as ever. Those who remember still speak glowingly of Penson's last production, "Montezuma."

The Historical Pageants were an unfailing source of excitement and pleasure to an audience unused to the sophisticated technical skills of film or daily television. Their message was always strongly patriotic and the moral a simple one — Good will triumph! Invariably, this moral ending took the form of pipers and soldiers, who swarmed over the field to save the day at the crucial moment.

Performers in the yearly pageants numbered into the thousands and were normally paid about $1.00 a day. Often they performed just for the thrill of it. Local schools of dance encouraged their students to participate as a means of both advertising and gaining experience. Since the capabilities and training of the dancers varied greatly, the choreography had to

be quite fundamental. But the over-all effect of the purely Canadian show moved the audience to heartfelt cheers year after year.

"Britannia," performed in 1941, was the last of these Historical Pageants. Canada was embroiled in World War II and the show was obviously a rallying cry to all members of the British Empire. The C.N.E. closed down for the remainder of the war and when it re-opened in 1947, the world had changed.

Fire destroyed the Grandstand in 1901 and again in 1946. Rebuilt for the 1948 season, its seating capacity was increased to the present 25,000. Meanwhile, verbal fireworks from the press and public over the quality of stars performing in front of the new grandstand threatened to scuttle the shows time and again.

For this new phase of the Grandstand shows, the directors of the C.N.E. appointed Leon Leonidoff as producer. He had been trained in Toronto and had then gone on to New York to successfully produce the famous shows at Radio City Music Hall. As he worked out of New York, he was chiefly acquainted with American performers. Thus, he engaged American package shows and dancers from the Rockettes' line to perform at the "EX." The dancers were augmented by a few Canadians. But the costumes, lighting, scenery, props and stage crew, indeed all the casts, were American.

It was Leonidoff who first introduced the popular Olsen and Johnson comedy team with their "Laffacade 1947." Although many people found the show entertaining, others in Toronto were extremely offended by it. Isobel Ross, Chairman of the Local Council of Women, was prevailed upon to attend a performance. The next day she described it to the press as being "vulgar, profane, indecent and an insult to womankind!"

Pressured by the C.N.E. Board of Directors, Olsen and Johnson promised to fumigate their act and they returned the next year with "Hellza Poppin." The Baptists denounced the show as "a moral outrage." Undaunted, "Hellza Poppin" went on to conquer the crowds at the "EX" and flourished even to the end of the 1951 season.

At this point the General Manager of the C.N.E., Elwood Hughes, decided to make some changes. Under constant pressure from the press and politicians to make the Grandstand shows more Canadian, Hughes contracted "Mr. Showbusiness," Jack Arthur.

As the new Producer, Jack Arthur was determined to present "a good show as economically as possible, utilizing native talent to the utmost." He assured people that Canadian acts would be competitive with foreign ones. American stars highlighted the shows because Arthur knew that very few Canadian acts had the experience necessary to attract large crowds or to cope with the difficulties of playing in a huge,

C.N.E. ARCHIVES

Chic Olsen and Olé Johnson

C.N.E. ARCHIVES

Danny Kaye headlined the 1950 show

open air stadium. Still, the balance of the show was Canadian. Besides the dancers and some of the individual acts, Canadians made up the stage crew, props and sets. And for the first time, all costumes were designed and supplied by a Toronto firm, Malabars.

One of Jack Arthur's outstanding contributions to the Grandstand shows was the clever choice of his attractive and talented wife, Midge, to choreograph and train the Canadettes. Lithe and lovely, the Canadettes were billed as the longest line of showgirls in the world.

During the first show of the Arthur era, staged in 1952, Midge worked with a veritable population of dancers; sixty women and twenty-four men. By 1967, budget restrictions threatened to cut the line too drastically. But Midge and her assistants, Natalya Butko and Jackie Couture, managed to produce an impressive display of chorus line work with only thirty-two dancers.

The dancers began practice three weeks before the "EX" opened. Rigorous rehearsals were held outside and everyone endured rain, cold, heat — one year the rubber actually melted off the soles of the dancers' shoes in the 110°F temperature. Seven hours a day of concentrated work, but all agreed it was worth it.

Sheila Billings, a former Miss Toronto, and Sandra O'Neill, the star of numerous musical reviews, were among some of the Canadette Alumnus destined for future recognition.

Training her dancers was a task that demanded both patience and originality. During the Canadettes' sixteen-year existence, Midge Arthur was responsible for teaching them the correct semaphore drill for a number that honoured the opening of the seaway. (The hundreds of sailors in the audience were obviously delighted.) She also took lessons in traffic signals from a constable. In fact, Midge drilled her girls so well that when they performed the police number, Toronto's Chief of police suggested that she might teach them to his men. She was just the sort of good-natured person to enjoy this kind of teasing. In spite of being a firm disciplinarian with her dancers, Midge Arthur's warm understanding made her loved and respected by all of them.

Working in close harmony, the Arthurs and the entire production team soon earned wide acclaim for the professional excellence of their shows. Alan and Blanche Lund, the renowned Canadian dance team, were responsible for the general choreography. And the fine musical arrangements flowed from the talent of Howard Cable.

Spectacle was the key to a good Grandstand Show, according to Jack Arthur. Each show was tied into a topical Canadian subject such as the opening of the Toronto Subway or the St. Lawrence Seaway. If nothing unusual had happened in Canada that year,

Midge Arthur's little dog broke up the Canadettes

then an international event was celebrated. Hugh Hand, by now President of the Hand Chemical Co., worked closely with Jack Arthur to produce a creative, dazzling effect in fireworks for each individual show.

Marilyn Bell, the first person to swim Lake Ontario, appeared in the Grandstand Show in 1955 — the year she completed the English Channel swim. For her part of the performance, she dove into a specially designed clear tank of water, twelve feet wide and sixty feet long. The audience greeted their heroine with wild enthusiasm.

Down through the years other Canadian performers made their appearance at the Grandstand shows. Max Ferguson portrayed his beloved character "old Rawhide," Celia Franca danced with the National Ballet, and the lovely soprano voice of Teresa Stratas throbbed over the stage as did the voice of the late Wally Koster, former singing star of "Cross Canada Hit Parade."

Stars were not always anxious to perform in the stadium. Its huge expanse and the trauma of giving open air performances could thoroughly unnerve the most seasoned veteran. Midge Arthur recalled going to Danny Kaye's dressingroom after his opening show. She found the star utterly dejected as he sat staring in the mirror. His act had bombed, or so he believed, for he hadn't been able to hear the audience's response. She reassured him that the au-

dience had indeed loved him, but that he had forgotten to allow for the time lapse between a comic line and its reaction across the vast audience. "Stop stepping on your laughs, Danny," she said. He followed her advice, and to everyone's enjoyment, the show worked beautifully.

One of the innovations of Jack Arthur's time was the building of a gigantic portable stage, at a cost of $500,000. It replaced the old stage that was rebuilt and dismantled at each season's close. The portable stage came in parts, which were carried on large caterpillars and hooked together when the stage was in position.

On one occasion, the stage had been laboriously moved from its rehearsal position at the end of the field to its show position; all the lighting stood arranged. The entire production staff decided to take a rest break in the trailer, parked only a few feet behind it. Moments later there was an earsplitting crash! Everyone rushed out of the trailer. The stage had slipped its moorings and gone rolling down the field to the other end of the stadium. It missed the trailer and its occupants by mere inches — and a mile of luck.

After sixteen years — they were often stormy, difficult years — Jack Arthur retired as the Grandstand show's producer in 1967. He had come to the position in his later years, topping an already impressive career with this final triumph. His retirement

C.N.E. ARCHIVES

C.N.E. ARCHIVES

The building of the gigantic portable stage

Jack Arthur surveys the construction

Packed to capacity

heralded the passing of an age in Grandstand entertainment.

The last pageant to be seen at the "EX" was "Sea to Sea," or "The Iron Miracle," in 1968. It was written by Don Harron and directed by David Yeddeau; Robert Christie, in his role as Sir John A. MacDonald, led a cast of 200 performers. Reactions to it were mixed. But there was one unforgettable moment when a glorious red and white balloon, representing the "Spirit of Canada," soared over the heads of the spectators.

The afternoon shows at the Grandstand that year offered a million thrills to the young, and not so young, who came to see Jack Kochman's "Hell Drivers" with their crazy daredevil motorcycle riding.

The end of the sixties and the balance of the seventies has produced a kaleidoscope of individual acts and well-known groups at the Grandstand — performers like Bob Hope, Bill Cosby, Anne Murray,

John Allan Cameron, Charley Pride, Bachman Turner Overdrive, the Beach Boys and many more.

Besides the Military Tattoos, often featuring the RCMP and their Musical Ride, the Grandstand has presented the National Drum and Bugle Corps Competitions, marching band spectaculars and folk-dancing festivals. One year saw the Circus International with 60 acts and seven rings. But the event guaranteed to fill the stadium with colour and music in the "Scottish World Festival Tattoo." It has returned to the "EX" every year since 1972, and always packs the Grandstand.

Styles and tastes change greatly during the passage of a century. What one generation found thrilling or fascinating often seems quaint to the next. Over the years the C.N.E. management has moved with the times and consistently offered the best value-packed entertainment that was available.

Scottish World Festival Tattoo

JAMES COLLECTION — CITY OF TORONTO ARCHIVES

MIKE FILEY COLLECTION

Communication

Left Hand Page: Interested onlookers watch demonstration of the Collins Wireless Telephone
Right Hand Page Top: Toronto Star Radio Building at C.N.E.
Bottom: Early Television sets

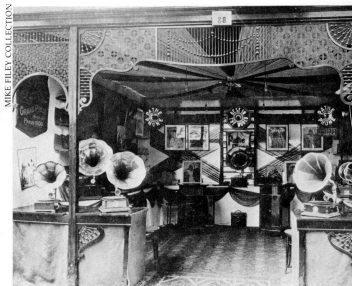

Phonograph display in music building and amphitheatre.

Covering the Marathon Race

An early telephone equipment display

"The Incredible Mrs. A"

by
Nancy Erb Kee

"The Incredible Mrs. 'A'!" people called her.

"She was keenly interested in everyone and remembered everything."

"A strong-minded, independent woman. Maybe she ruffled a few feathers on occasion – but she got things done!"

"They loved her. She worked herself and her staff like mad, but they loved her."

These are just a few of the semtiments likely to be expressed when people speak about Kate Aitken – the lively

These are just a few of the sentiments likely to be expressed when people speak about Kate Aitken — the lively, imaginative woman whose association with the CNE lasted for nearly thirty years. Under her direction thousands of women, and more than a few men, were stimulated to new heights in the art of homemaking and cooking. They learned much and were thoroughly entertained at the same time.

She was the very essence of the perfect homemaker. Bright and practical, with a great sense of fun. Her style inspired people all across the country to

Left: Mrs. Aitken demonstrates the canning of fruits, vegetables, meat and poultry in small farm kitchen set up in the west wing of women's building

Right: Mrs. Aitken

explore new ways of making ends meet and improving their brilliant hospitality. Mrs. 'A's *brilliant* years as head of the CNE Women's Division are remembered to this day.

Kate Aitken's association with the "EX" began in a modest way. From her own trips to the Fair she concluded that what the CNE really needed was an old-fashioned country kitchen. In 1923, she leased about ten square feet from the management and set up her exhibit in the Women's Building. She filled her Country Kitchen with delicious jams and jellies and pickles. The mouth watered over her daily stock of fresh home-baked rolls, cakes, pies. And for the eye, she arranged a collection of handsome quilts and handicrafts.

Her exhibit and demonstrations of cooking proved instantly popular. Women, who often felt cooly indifferent to the sight of prize bulls or the latest machinery, flocked to the Country Kitchen for that homely touch. They were captivated by Mrs. 'A's warmth and her practical tips on canning and preserving.

The outstanding success of her first venture led to a proposal by CNE directors that Mrs. 'A' conduct a cooking school on the grounds. They felt her personality and obvious capabilities were just right for the job. Never one to say "no" to an interesting opportunity, Kate Aitken agreed and an area in the Fashion Court of the old Women's Building was set aside for her demonstrations. By 1927, her enthusiastic audiences filled the entire building for every show.

Although Mrs. 'A' had never been formally trained in the culinary arts, she came to the task with a wealth of practical experience. Being the eldest girl in a family of boys, she had learned about efficiency in the kitchen from her mother's hurried examples. Here was the source of her ability to at once carry on a conversation while swiftly preparing food. Besides these attributes, she had successfully run a "Cottage industry" of preserving and canning fruit and poultry on a family farm at Beeton, Ontario. Yearly her farm managed to produce 12,000 jars and cans of food. These were sought by and sold to specialty shops in Toronto.

Mrs. 'A's' cooking school was preceded by a grand fashion show, complete with lavish background. Models swept down a golden staircase and paraded the latest fashions, which usually included a final, flowery bridal scene. The cooking school's problem was to switch the audience from this mood of "O Perfect Love" to "Home on the Range."

It was done in the wink of an eye. As the stage crew wheeled the gold staircase into the left wing, preheated stoves, refrigerators and kitchen tables were moving into place from the right. The sink and cupboards were carried on stage and then the background appeared with its frilly-curtained window and potted geraniums. It seemed almost magical.

But there were some real hazards encountered during these cooking demonstrations. Most of the diffi-

Women in costume at the Exhibition 1929

The Hornby Ladies make tea in the picture used to publicize the early Canadian fashion show for the C.N.E.

Women in old costume at the Exhibition 1927

culty had to do with the old building, which lacked the proper facilities for electricity and plumbing. To feed the stoves and refrigerators, electric cables were laid in snaking lengths along the stage floor. It required some pretty fast footwork on Mrs. 'A's part to step over them casually, without a downward glance, and not fall flat on her face.

Another major problem was created by cold water drainage from the sink. To overcome it, the head plumber laid in a dry well under the stage. Every time the sink was fitted in place, a plumber had to make certain the rubber tubing was clear between sink and dry well. He did this by crawling under the stage and blowing up through the tubing. Once, when he was still puffing and blowing, an assistant turned on the stage tap full force. Mrs. 'A' did her best to ignore the strong language issuing from below stage as she "calmly" went on making an elegant party dish.

All this changed when the new Electrical Building was completed. The manufacturers of kitchen appliances asked Mrs. 'A' to move her cooking school to their building. They felt it would be a natural drawing card for potential customers.

She readily accepted and found herself in a delightful theatre set in the heart of the building. Her position was flanked by aisles of competitive stoves, refrigerators, washing machines and all manner of electrical appliances. To the audience, seated (12,000 strong) in a semicircle round the auditorium, the theatre seemed a bright and friendly place. Its white-painted walls reflected the sunny tones of a billowing dropped ceiling done in cottons of daffodil-yellow.

The stage was adequate. And for a change, the prep kitchens had so many stoves and refrigerators, that Mrs. 'A' and her staff could hardly find their way among them.

Her staff of twelve included ten university students, both male and female. They were a cheerful, eager bunch of young people who undertook any type of work from sweeping out the theatre to peeling the vegetables. They even licked the cake bowls clean.

Part of their duties required them to change into "whites" just before the 2:00 pm show. Freshly dressed, they seated the audience and handed out programmes. Then they dashed off to change into costumes for the stage and radio show that was broadcast daily during the cooking school intermission.

During each afternoon and evening cooking school many product prizes were given away, as were the items baked on the show. But it was the three special prizes that really worked up the audience's interest. Often with amusing results. One prize was a silver plate awarded to the newest bride. Another was an engraved silver tray for the person who had come the greatest distance and the third was a beautiful three-tiered birthday cake destined for the oldest person in the audience.

Long-distance travellers were delighted by the handsome silver tray and even took to wrangling with each other about mileage, the routes taken and so on. In the interests of peace, the show installed a large-scale map of the world and a steel rule to silence the arguments in the audience.

Similarly, the large birthday cake, borne on stage with its candles aglow, always seemed to prompt anyone over seventy to add years to his or her age. On one show, the cake finally had to be cut in half as neither recipient would admit to being one minute younger than the other.

The directors of the Exhibition realized that the whole field of women's interests could be expanded

Eldest lady in the audience wins the cake.

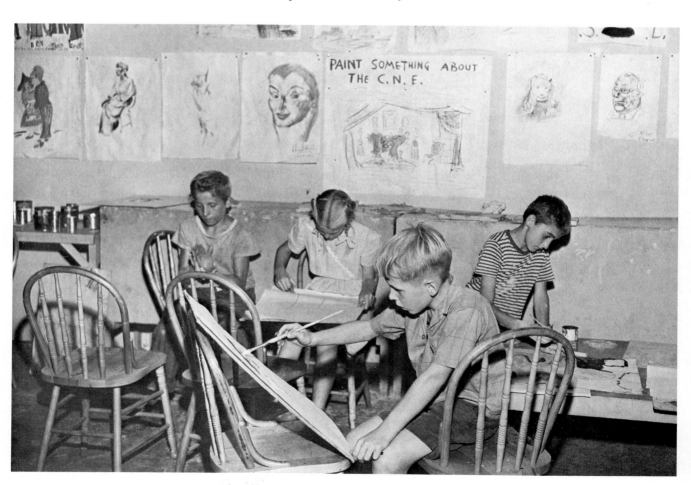

and improved to broaden its appeal and draw larger crowds. Quite naturally, they turned to Kate Aitken. With her highly successful cooking schools and broadcasts, she was just the person to revitalize the entire Women's Division. Thus, in 1938, Mrs. 'A' was made Director of Women's Activities for the CNE.

She did not assume these duties lightly. Kate Aitkin also worked on a full-time contract for the Tamblyn drug chain. Normally, she worked from Tamblyn's head office on Jarvis Street in Toronto, but every April she moved her entire staff (including nine secretaries) to the Women's Building on the Exhibition grounds. From April until the "EX" closed down after Labour Day, Mrs. Aitken and her staff worked full tilt. Arrangements had to be made for her two daily broadcasts, her newspaper articles and the organization of the Women's Division.

As the days grew nearer to the opening of the "EX," the pace quickened dramatically. Blueprints were constantly altered and last minute thoughts disrupted the best laid plans.

Amazing, but everything was actually ready by 6:00 am on the opening day. The exhausted staff had finished their preparations and were sitting down to breakfast. When the big gates opened at 9:00 am everything was as fresh as a new penny, and the manufacturers and crowds were delighted.

Volunteer women sewing for bombed-out Britain at the C.N.E. 1941

Popular features of the Women's Division were, and still are, the school arts and handicraft displays. One of the chief judges of the handicrafts for many years was Miss Helen Creighton. She was head of the Home Economics Department of Central Technical School in Toronto, and many considered her an expert in the field of sewing, knitting and group coordination.

It was to Miss Creighton that Mrs. 'A' turned in 1941, when the "EX" opened for its season. World War II had Britain staggering under heavy bombardment; many areas of her fine cities were being reduced to rubble and her citizens left destitute. Help was needed badly. A hundred old treadle sewing machines were set up in the Women's Division and

each day, under Miss Creighton's direction, a different group of women from the various volunteer organizations in Ontario came to the "EX" to sew clothes for the bombed-out British. They concentrated on trying to supply the clothing needs of a different city every day of the fair. One day they worked for Coventry, the next for Plymouth and so on through the roster.

People were very interested in the women's war work and flocked to the area, where flags and signs proclaimed what was happening.

The Duke of Kent officially opened the CNE that year and asked to see the site. Apparently, Mrs. 'A' tried to introduce the hardpressed Miss Creighton to the Duke. With a perfunctory, "How do you do," Miss Creighton turned back to Kate Aitken. "Now, Mrs. 'A', about fifty of these old machines aren't working properly and something must be done about them."

Mrs. 'A' said gently, "Miss Creighton, I'm trying to present you to the Duke of Kent."

"How do you do," Miss Creighton repeated. "Really, Mrs. 'A', you must do something about these machines. We simply can't go on producing efficiently under these circumstances."

A third attempt at an introduction produced the same results and the Duke burst out laughing. He simply couldn't compete with the singular importance of fifty broken-down old treadle machines.

Every afternoon and every evening, Mrs. 'A' did one-hour broadcasts live from the Coliseum at the CNE. Her shows included interviews with some of the famous personalities who were visiting the Exhibition that day, as well as news and travel tips.

Cy Strange, of the CBC, was the announcer on these shows and Horace Lapp played the organ. He provided mood music and the bridges from one item to the next. Every move had to be timed perfectly for the radio transmission. Horace Lapp recalled one particular show. The producer was telling an audience at the cooking demonstration about the vital need for everything to be timed to the split second — not a moment could be lost. At which point, he waved his arm and knocked over a bottle of milk. It splashed out everywhere and a good many of those precious split seconds were lost to the mop and pail.

Mrs. Aitken's ability to organize things was amply demonstrated in her running of three restaurants at the CNE. They did all their own catering and she was responsible for the entire operation. Her chief pleasure was in arranging the daily luncheons for the 200 invited guests from industry, the professions and other organizations. On the Press, Radio and TV Day, luncheon was prepared for 600 guests.

They were elegant affairs held on the private balcony of the Women's Building. Mrs. 'A' frequently taped interviews with her guests and used them later in her broadcasts. Among some of the more famous women Mrs. 'A' entertained were Queen Juliana of the Netherlands, Countess Mountbatten and the gentle Lady Alexander. America's beloved first lady, Mrs. Eleanor Roosevelt, was one luncheon guest whose words became part of the great moments in radio.

Even as Mrs. 'A' *addressed* her radio listeners, she was conscious of the other programmes being presented to audiences at CNE. Three theatres provided continuous entertainment from 1:00 pm to 10:00 pm. the fare had to be varied to suit the tastes of different audiences, but the main theme of all the shows was the "Capture, Care and Feeding of Husbands." The thirty-seven fashion shows presented each day furnished inspiration for the "Capture" and were always packed. Mrs. Aitken often did the commentating while Horace Lapp played the piano for the models as they swept down the runway. Fur coats were very popular with the audience, even though the models nearly melted in the August heat.

There were daily demonstrations staged on the theme of "Exercise and Stay Slim." The audience was usually invited to participate with these words: "Now ladies, here is an easy exercise in which you can join without having to stand up. Stretch both arms up straight; breathe deeply, now lift... lift ... lift..." In spite of popped buttons, burst zippers and split seams, the audience invariably seemed to want more.

Different competitions were held each day of the Fair and became a great source of interest for many Exhibition visitors. Octogenarians seemed especially drawn to them and often entered every competition just for the fun of it. Some of the contests included trimming hats, spelling or making furniture out of

Lord Alexander officially opens C.N.E. Receiving on bandshell, Mrs. A. presents girl student from Newfoundland

orange crates. The cash prizes offered were high enough to attract large numbers of entrants. With its prize of $100, the Newscaster Competition appealed to amateurs and professionals alike.

One year a typing contest was held, open to men only. It revealed some surprisingly efficient typists. Another year Mrs. 'A' decided to hold an Early Canadian Fashion Show. Some of the ladies from the Women's Institute of Hornby, Ontario, were asked to model the costumes they had found in their attics. The resulting photographs were used to publicize the event. In dress and bearing the Unionville Institute woman who captured first prize was the exact image of Queen Victoria.

$10,000 suit

Exercises "Stay Slim"
demonstrations were very popular

Mrs. McFarlane with her collection of historical dolls

Mrs. R. Perkin modelling an early Canadian's bride's dress, curtseying
to the Queen. Mrs. McRae is wearing one of Queen Victoria's gowns

But the year Mrs. 'A' thought of sponsoring the "Canadiana" competition will stand long in the memory of anyone connected with it. People were asked to send along any bits and pieces associated with pioneer life. These were to be well-labelled so that they could be returned. "An extraordinary assortment of "Canadiana" poured into the display at the Coliseum. The idea was to try to guess what everything was and its use. The collection included beautiful old rolling pins, mangles, butter presses and something that kept everyone guessing for ages. It turned out to be a heavy iron used for crimping petticoats.

When the competition was finished, everything had to be returned to the owners. Then the trouble began. The person in charge of the event had had a casual attitude toward the whole affair and somehow all the labels had been muddled. People phoned the CNE for days to complain about such things as mangles being returned instead of great-grandmother's clothes press and others complained that they'd received the wrong rolling pins. Those who had sent in their old washing machines told the CNE to keep them. Finally, weeks later, everything was straightened out satisfactorily.

The home baking competitions were the most fiercely contested of all. In Kate Aitken's day, the contestants were usually women and they took a deep pride in turning out the moistest cakes and the tastiest pies in the country. One woman, who had year after year won first prize for her butter tarts, finally went down to defeat. As she watched the first, second and third ribbons being awarded, she suddenly realized she wasn't even to receive a consolation prize. With a cry of "Take that and that!" she angrily dumped her tray of butter tarts over the bald head of the chief judge. Syrup, pastry, raisins and nuts slid down his face and over his white smock. The crowd stood dumbfounded.

The competition that really caused a stir occurred in 1948. That was the year Kate Aitken decided to hold a beauty contest. Admittedly, there wasn't anything very startling in the idea — until Mrs. 'A' revealed it was to be a contest for young men. Furthermore, it would be judged by several young ladies who were gaining recognition in the city. Toby Robins was one. She later went on to theatre and TV fame, but in 1948 she was Miss Canadian Exhibition.

On the day of the contest, dozens of young men arrived on the scene clad in conservative business

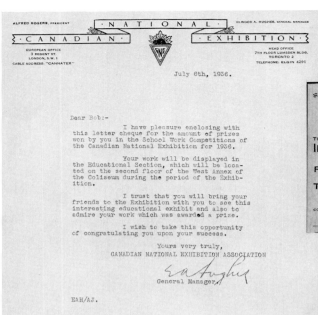

suits or sports clothes. They paraded before the judges and were duly examined, down to the finalists. These contestants changed into skimpy bathing suits and once more were thoroughly scrutinized by the judges. At last the winner was announced and Toby Robins kissed him for the newsmen and cameras. That was the end of it, or so everyone thought.

The next day, however, Mrs. 'A' was roundly criticized in the press for allowing innocent young ladies to study the male figure in such a fashion. Kate Aitken remained unperturbed. She always knew what she was doing.

By 1952, the Women's Division had grown to such mammoth proportions that Mrs. 'A' finally decided to resign and let other people take on the job. She had loved the "EX" for many years and had contributed an enormous amount of time, energy and thought to it. She resigned after the big gates closed at the end of the 1952 season. In her farewell speech she observed, "Nowhere in the world can you meet people from all walks of life as you can at the "EX." the CNE is the great Canadian democracy in action."

Elwood Hughes, General Manager of the CNE at the time, wondered aloud, "Where on earth will we find a replacement for Kate Aitken?" He and his directors carefully studied all the applications for the onerous position. They finally chose Elsa Jenkins. She took over the post the following season and has been firmly in command of the Women's Division and the Better Living Centre for the past twenty-five years.

She had a wide range of experience before she accepted the CNE assignment. Reporter for the Globe and Mail and then an editor of Style magazine, Elsa continued to distinguish herself by becoming CBC's first woman announcer.

Mrs. Jenkin's bright smile and comfortable manner has literally put thousands of people at their ease. Her attention must be spread over contestants, exhibitors, the public and the media, and the hundreds of situations that crop up in her fascinating job.

The Women's Division has expanded steadily over the years and new ideas have been constantly introduced. The old Women's Building, which burned down in 1961, has been replaced by the huge, airy Better Living Centre, built in 1962, at a cost of $3,500,000. It houses all the concerns in the division with the exception of the large fashion shows.

Immigration to Canada and widespread travel have made a great impact on the CNE in the last twenty-five years. This is particularly noticeable in the Kitchen Theatre, where food experts of different nationalities cook and demonstrate a variety of exotic and tempting dishes.

Folk dancers, representing the countries that now make up Canada's mosaic, perform nightly in front of the Better Living Centre. Dressed in their native cos-

tume, they add a colourful worldliness to the Exhibition.

Baking competitions and handicrafts, which thirty years ago were sole domain of women, are now entered by young people of both sexes. From cities and towns. And elderly men, with more time to discover the joy of doing something creative, are now swelling the ranks of participants.

Materials, too, have changed, offering more opportunity to experiment with new effects. The crafts on display today at the CNE have attained a very high standard.

The school arts entries start pouring into the CNE by mid-April. Close to 3,000 entries come from all parts of Canada — from Frobisher Bay, NWT, to Cornerbrook, Newfoundland. They point out the national scope of the Exhibition. Cash prizes are awarded to the best in murals, penmanship and creative writing. The range of materials used and the talent displayed are quite a revelation to those unused to children's work. All the selections are displayed in the Better Living Centre.

A recent innovation of Mrs. Jenkins has been the extremely successful Film Competition and Festival. Open to all post-secondary students in Canada, its purpose is to encourage them to develop and pursue their interest in film making. Certificates, cash prizes and awards of merit are the plums to be won. As an added incentive, this year's prize winning films may as were last year's be invited to participate in the International Hong Kong Film Festival.

To handle the manifold duties of the Women's Division, Elsa Jenkins relies on a strong support staff, which swells to about 100 during the Exhibition.

Some of her staff members have been with the division since the early fifties and their devotion to the "EX" shows in their work. Barbara Maskell remembers the days when she had to type 100 letters a day for Mrs. 'A'. Recently, she helped to handle the preparations for the 2,000 guests who attended the beautiful Centennial Ball, thrown by the CNE.

Maria Rahmer de Nagay, a sculptor and designer, has also worked in the division since the early fifties. In designing the furnished rooms for the manufacturers, she has noted the transitions in styles and attitudes over the years. Today the manufacturers place more emphasis on each detail in their displays than they did twenty years ago.

The Women's Division has come a long way since the days when Kate Aitken was first asked to apply her inventive mind and boundless energy to the task of expanding it. The women responsible for it have needed the courage to try new ideas and to persevere, while dealing amicably with a multitude of people. In short, they have had to be good executives. Both Kate Aitken and Elsa Jenkins have demonstrated these exceptional qualities. As a result, the Women's Division is an area of which the Canadian National Exhibition can be justly proud.

ER SPORTS
RUBIN & CHERRY
PRESENTS
SHIRLEY FRANCES
BEACH STYLE REVUE
NEPTUNE'S DAUGHTERS
GH & FA Y D ER

Midway Magic

by
John Downing

They say the midway began at Chicago's World Fair in 1893. Only the modern version did. The midway's roots go much deeper. They grow out of man's desire to laugh, gamble and dream, the wish to dazzle senses and wonder at the world and its more exotic offspring.

The midway really began once we left the caves behind, and that desperate daily scramble for life, and could gather in markets, fairs and celebrations. There were geeks, gimmicks, gamblers and games throughout history. Strongmen to taunt challengers! Strange animals from hot lands!

It's comforting and familiar to read of the "glee men" at a Merrie Olde England Fair in 1133 during the reign of the first Henry. There were dancers, posturers, jugglers, tumblers, and exhibitors of performing animals, we're told. We didn't call them glee men but carnies and showmen at the first Ex', and the 50th, and they'll probably be with us a century from now, although the animals and games may be from

Left: Hurry, hurry . . .for the time of your life

Muscle powered ferris wheel c. 1892

C.N.E. Circus lady (1910)

other worlds. The more things change, the more they are the same.

The little fair got underway in its permanent home in 1879 without a midway. But then, the name and concept hadn't been invented. There were sideshows in tiny tents, with their curiosities, fantasies and thrills. But they were scattered throughout, not clumped in a magnet for the kids, and those who would still like to be.

The first ride was a muscle-powered Ferris wheel. But that word hadn't been invented either when it spun in 1879 or the early 1880s. No one is sure exactly when. It held eight people in four seats and swung them a death-defying 15 or so giddy feet above the ground. Head spinning!

It was a tiny step forward for a ride which was to become a midway favourite — after the ride and midway got invented, that is. That came when The Man With Wheels In His Head, George Washington Gale Ferris, chugged his steam-driven wheel into action at the Chicago Fair and became a household word.

The wheels were to become the midways' barometers. You could tell how business was by looking up to see if the Ferris or "Big Eli" wheels were full.

But let's not skip ahead. This is still the early days, when the only flash and sizzle of colored lights overhead came from fireworks, not huffing, puffing mechanical fun merchants. William Hand, a professor naturally, got his company underway in 1873. His fireworks and the Ex would have a love affair for a century. If it wasn't The Burning of Rome in pyrotechnic splendor, it was The Relief of Locknow or rockets exploding in air with a thump that makes the hair rise. That's was they wanted to do in the sideshows, too, but fireworks appealed to more senses.

To regain some of the Ex's earliest history, you harvest tiny programs with gay covers, each about three inches by five inches. The booklet tells us in 1887 that the crowd flocked to see Queen Victoria in her Jubilee robes. In case you wondered, the great queen really wasn't there, but a wax model was.

There were thrilling balloon races and ascensions into the heights. The men always had names starting with Professor, and the helpers were fair, young maidens with a Miss in front of theirs.

The wonders of sideshows had to compete with the inventions of a golden age of progress. When one lit bulb was a marvel, people were tantalized with "great illuminations nightly with 200 electric arc lights." Later, there would be that many on most rides. The big ride wasn't even a midway one but the crowd goggled over an "electric railway". Oh yes, in true midway style, that program offered: "Great mechanical wonders and automatic novelties, instructive and interesting, and many other features now being arranged for." Now there's a midway touch — tantalizing with delicious hints of more, much more.

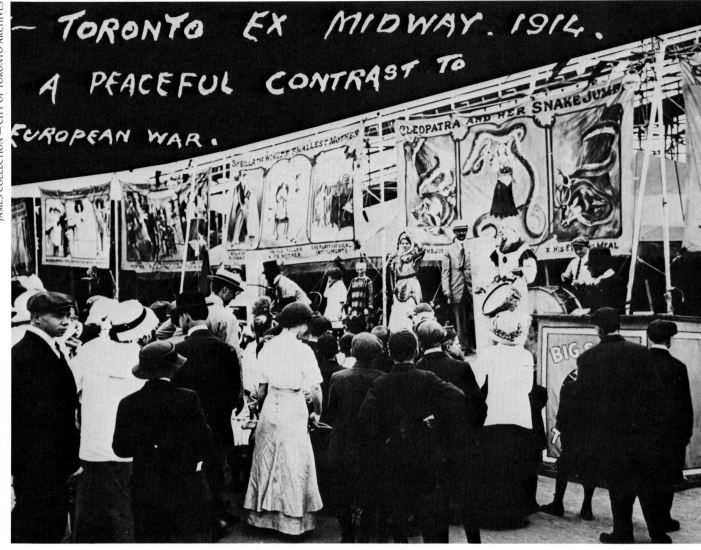

The midway 1914

Midway bathing beauties 1920

Sideshow performers C 1914

Sideshows continued to compete with the new wonders of science and inventors. In 1888, people marvelled at Muncasey's "great $100,000 picture Christ Before Pilate." But a rival attraction was Edison's latest and most wonderful invention, the Perfected Phonograph.

The new world for fair entertainment arrived in 1893 at the Chicago World's Fair. For the first time, the authorities set aside just one area for what they called the curiousities, fantasies and scenes from foreign life. The name for the area was Midway Plaisance. In its shortened form, a magic word was born. That same fair brought the world the idea of travelling companies of showmen, not just each outfit making its lonely way.

The showmen had converged early on Chicago, to woo the dollars from the thousands of workmen building the fair. When the fair began, many clustered around the big attraction of Buffalo Bill's Wild West Show, hoping to catch some of the business. It was the first time they had worked in the same spot for a long period. And the idea was born that if their shows, games and riding devices banded together and moved from fair to fair they would be an even bigger attraction.

The Chicago fair lasted for three years. But it didn't take that long for the message to reach Toronto. Rides were popular in Chicago. So let's have them in Toronto, and advertise them. In 1894, the program promised "Ferris Wheels, Carousals, Swings and other amusements for young and old."

There was an added note, proof of the cynicism that fair officials and the newspapers would show to the entire amusement side of the Ex' over the years. At one of the Toronto Fairs held before the Ex', a newspaper warned about the tents and booths that are being raised to turn "an honest penny and, it is feared, some dishonest ones also. In this booth will be sold intoxicating liquors, and in that, jugglers and thimbleriggers will doubtless ply their nefarious trades. Thieves, pickpockets, gamblers, swindlers and vagabonds may be expected to hold forth in the neighbourhood of the main gate, and subsequently it is to be hoped a large number of detectives will be kept in that quarter to look after them and protect the unwary citizens or credulous countrymen from being fleeced by those who live by picking and stealing." In 1894 the program warned "The Association will not permit gambling, fakirs and any other objectionable feature on the grounds."

Rides at the C.N.E. (1928)

What was allowed was the fireworks spectacular, The Siege of Algiers, "with over 400 people, introducing ships of war, troops and marines, calvary and artillery in actual combat." Direct from Cologne, Germany came the very latest attraction, Living Pictures — A beautiful combination of art and science, presented with wonderful electrical effects, magnificent reproductions of the great works of art."

There was more, much more. Phantasmagoric views, a minstrel show called In Days Of Slavery. Monster balloon ascensions by Prof. Woolcott and Miss Lamount. The California Phantom Car. And Edison's latest invention, the Kinetoscope.

In 1899, the Ex' copied Chicago's complete idea but tried a different name. The program reported: "To the south of the road leading from the Main Building to the Grand Stand will be located 'The Olio-de-Plaisance', or in plain English, 'The Place of Amusement.' It will be totally superior to most of the somewhat similar features known as 'Midways', inasmuch as it will be directly under the supervision of the Exposition management, and all the shows alloted space therein have been considered of sufficient merit to warrant them being given space on the grounds. No feature that could be considered objectionable from any standpoint has been admitted, and the public who desire to patronize this interesting feature of the Exposition can depend upon 'getting their money's worth'."

So what did you get for your money as the last century ended?

If you went to 'The Plaisance', as officials hoped it would be called, you would find the lions, leopards, kangaroos, monkeys, elephants and camels of Hagenback's trained wild animal exhibition. You would also find freaks. For years, the aim was to have something better than those first living Siamese twins, Chang and Eng, who had died in 1874 but not before they had become known throughout the world.

In 1893, the Ex' had a two-headed boy which was billed as better than the twins. Now, in 1899, it was "Millie Christine, the Carolina twins, the greatest psychological wonder of the entire world and undoubtedly the only rival to the famous Siamese twins." The Ex' had Chiquita, "the living doll, smallest lady in the world." And Willie Stout, the Texas fat boy, one of the biggest people.

There was an Indian village, Turkish theatre, Chinese theatre, Japanese theatre and Prof. Pepper's London ghost show and other illusions.

But the biggest illusion was to be found on the silver screen. "Lumiere's Marvelous Cinematographe with an entirely new departure just imported from France especially for the Exposition, including the mysterious series, the Laboratory of Mephistopheles, the Man in the Moon, Pygmalion and Galates, the man with four heads, the Mysterious Dinner Party, English and American military and other scenes etc.,

Hollywood Chimp Show 1937

the best moving picture show ever presented in Canada."

When the Cinematographe had so much to offer, no wonder it was a big money maker. In 1896, the Ex' received $1,300 as its share of receipts, more than it got from the wax works, electric science theatre or hexirograph.

By 1902, 'The Plaisance' name had faded and the annual report was explaining that because of complaints from exhibitors "regarding the placing of side-shows throughout the grounds, your board last year decided to concentrate them all into one 'Midway' at the eastern end of the Grand Stand."

The Midway had its home and its name. The board said grouping the entertainment worked so well, it should continue. Typically, the board also snarled a bit. It endeavoured to "see that only shows in keeping with the standing of the Exposition were allowed in the Midway" but it found one violating this standard and ordered it closed.

The pattern was set. This was where the double roller coaster would be built and the touring rides located. The tents would line a street flooded with people gawking at fierce men challenging anyone to go a round. There were people swallowing fire and swords amd stomach turning things. There were seductive pitches about the soft wonders of the veiled dancers within. So the people thronged inside, and kids tried to sneak in under the back, only to be greeted by a rough boot. In 1905, the Ex's chairman harrumped that the midway had no features that could be considered objectionable but "your directors did find it necessary on account of the language used by the spielers in front of some of these shows, to close them. We cannot have this sort of thing at the exhibition."

Someone who loved alliteration called the midway the mystic mile of merriment. Whatever you wanted to call it, it slowly grew and grew. Much of it was raw and crude by modern standards. But some was familiar. After all, there are only so many things you can do with water. And they've been doing it through the decades at the Ex's. High Tower divers plunged sickeningly towards tiny pools in 1895, and they did it at recent Ex's. There have always been "fancy swimmers, tub races and log rolling contests."

The midway constantly added to its honky tonk glitter as it found new ways to put hearts in mouth and hands in purses. Still, there was not the present bewildering selections of thrill rides. As late as 1920, the typical carnival had only three rides: a whip, a merry-go-round and a Ferris wheel. Ex-goers were luckier. In 1910, it had "The Gorge, Ferris wheel, merry-go-round, Chute The Chutes and Roller Boller Coaster." Only nine years later, the Ex' boasted on doubled fun, with two Ferris wheels, two whips and two carousals, spelled regularly without an "e". There were also rides called the Frolic and Over The

Some of the lucky boys on the ''Front End'' (the lineup of gaming concessions was always called the front end)

Falls. Still, the heart of the early midway continued to be the sideshows.

The strange animals and Wild West extravaganzas, midgets, tall people and fat people, glass blowing and vaudeville shows. Dogs and horses did tricks, pretty girls wiggled and giggled and men squinted down rifles in one last attempt to win a kewpie doll for the admiring girlfriend.

Capturing the midway's essence in print is as difficult and elusive a task as finding the substance in cotton candy, or catching the drips from a cone when it's 100 degrees and there's no breeze off the lake. It's greed and guile and sounds and smells and thrills wrapped into one delightful heaven for kids. It's their Ex. They can see the rest when they're broke.

George Kidd, a veteran journalist who loves the Ex, has written about the search for the free ticket that the teacher had given you weeks before, and then the anxious trip to the grounds for Children's Day.

You just give a glance at Society Row to your right and then rush through the Women's Building. Then past the fountain and a quick detour through the Manufacturer's Building, hoping for a free sample. Then the mad rush past the Grand Stand and there it is . . . the midway. At this age you really don't know too much about paradise but all of a sudden you know that this is IT. Everything is in motion. You get a whiff of onions and hot dogs and pop corn and hamburgers and you hear the crazy sounds all mingl-

ing with each other to form a giant but discordant symphony. The shouts from the barkers form a special kind of chorus, and high above you the screams of kids join in as they take that terrifying plunge on the roller coaster. . . ."

Ted Reeve, that beloved bard of the Beaches, has written with warmth about his visits "on faraway golden August days." Of sounds like the beautiful brass of bands, the "thumpety-thump of that expectancy music of the calliopes," and "the hoarse voiced engagingly larcenous spielers . . . appealing to the gazers to come, come and see The Wild Man from Borneo who was captured at tremendous loss of life." Of sights like the tattoed lady, with a thousand marks on her anatomy, and Eno the Turtle Boy, "the boneless wondah who eats, drinks and sleeps like you and I but UNDAH watah."

Memories! Daring your chum to ride the gut-churning twister; Swigs of cool Honey Dew. Mustard drooling from a Ritz Carlton Red Hot. A crane's claws dropping the nicest bit of loot in the case just before you had it. The huge stuffed panda you didn't expect to win . . . and the time you couldn't win no matter how hard you tried for HER! Your name stamped on soft metal. Going into sympathetic hysterics as you watch the laughing lady halfway down the midway. Trying to sneak a free glance inside sideshows after all your money has trickled away. Nice memories!

Not everyone loves the midway or its carnies and owners. There have been drastic changes over the

Student actors present skits, songs and dances of the 1920's at Conklins Antique Carnival 1978

years. Changing values dictated that there was something depraved about gawking at adults and children that nature had cruelly distorted. So freak shows went and we watched instead war on the evening news. Many of the early games of chance or skill were fixed — or as the carnies said in their colorful slang, gaffed. That cut down on the "hard flash" that had to be given away, slang for prizes like radios or vacuum cleaners. There were "flat stores" where no one ever won anything from the tempting rows of prizes. But they're gone. They disappeared along with the Alaskan ice worms and two-headed babies, and that fierce pygmy from darkest Africa who really was a midget you saw downtown the rest of the year. Now the attitude of the midway is let the customers win.

That's the best advertisement. That keeps them coming back. And at least a third of the time, the customer does win.

Sometimes it's not the prize that counts but the winning. Logic is suspended by fun. It's fun to beat the weight guesser. The prize often isn't worth the cost.

It was fun to snap the wrists and hammer and make the bell ring when brawny chaps sometimes failed, to the snickers of the crowd. It was fun to stop your coin so cleverly on the plate, although what you were going to do with that plate, you weren't quite sure. Kids who hadn't taken their teddy to bed for years went saucer-eyed on winning one, or two, or three.

Another Winner!

But for some of you, your mecca is the thrill rides. Not the more sedate wheels or merry-go-rounds, but the descendents of the ship developed in Coney Island in 1915. It lures and terrifies with that sensation of being hurtled around the very edges of safety. You can see its offspring as you walk the empire of Canada's Conklin Shows. Patty Conklin won the right to provide the Ex's midway in 1937 after several years of trying. It meant the end at the Ex of another familiar fair name, the giant Rubin & Cherry Shows of Rubin Gruberg. Ex directors were reluctant to see Gruberg go. But Conklin made them forget. Conklin built on his success with innovations and hard work. He believed in not gaffing the customer but giving him an even break. It brought him prosperity, and happiness, if not a prize, for the players.

Conklin brought "new and novel riding devices", as he advertised each year, until the hot air seemed to hum with clatter and swooshes. That is, if you could hear the mirth machines over the screams and laughter that showered out of them.

Some don't see the smile on the midway's face, just how grubby, sweaty and smelly it can be with a huge crowd. Sure it's that way sometimes, just like the face of a kid having a grand time. For many, the midway IS the Ex, a place for a final fling after the summer holidays.

You cannot capture its ingredients any more than you can split fun. It's to be enjoyed, not analysed.

Armed Forces

A Great Military Camp

By Dr. Oswald C. V. Withrow

August 4th, 1914 found Canada anxious with the other members of the British Empire, to do her part in the war that day declared. She began at once to mobilize troops and train them for overseas service.

In those stirring days barracks had to be found for thousands upon thousands of citizen soldiers, since the permanent military garrisons of Canada were not many or large.

The Directors of the Canadian National Exhibition gladly offered Exhibition Park with its numerous large permanent buildings to Military District Number Two for use as a barracks during the winter months as long as the war should continue. As a matter of fact the troops were accommodated during the winters of 1914, 1915 and 1916.

Left Page: Review of the regulars by Prince Arthur of Connaught at Stanley Barracks 1841
Mike Filey Collection

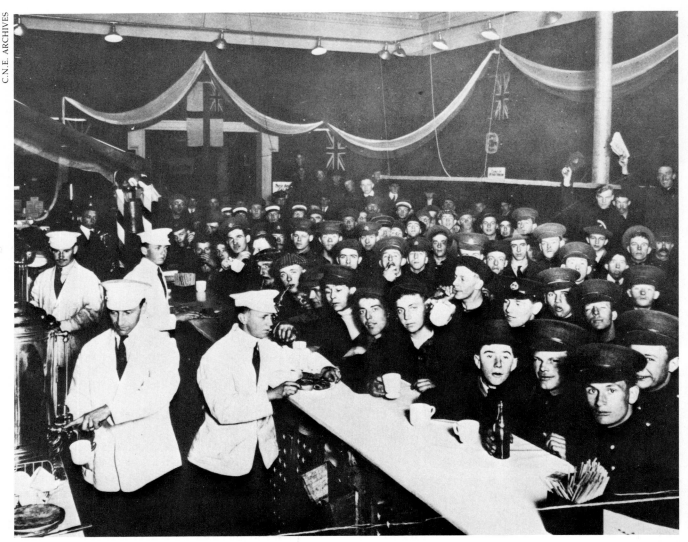

Army Canteen 1915

The Exhibition was able to carry on during each of the war years on the usual dates, for the troops were then under canvas at Niagara-on-the-Lake, but when the chilly blasts came the citizen soldiers were housed snug and warm in the permanent structures at Exhibition Park.

Double-decker bunks were placed in all the buildings and sufficient huge stoves were installed to make them comfortable.

The Women's building and part of the Manufacturers' Building were utilized as the camp hospital, completely equipped for performing the most intricate surgery and for administering the most up-to-date treatments.

The Administration building was chosen as Headquarters from which the G.O.C. commanded at times as many as 15,000 soldiers within the Park alone.

To mention a few of the units during one winter season: the 74th occupied the Government Building, the 75th the Horticultural, the 95th and 97th (American Battalion) shared the Process Building, and the

81st was in the Poultry Building, having taken over the lines from the 58th. Details of all arms of the service were scattered here and there among the stables.

Can anyone ever forget the November of 1915 when unit after unit, on successive days, left the camp at Niagara-on-the-Lake for a trek of one hundred miles on six marching days to Toronto and Exhibition Camp?

During the Exhibition of 1915, picked men from the 35th Battalion C.E.F. gave marvellous drill and athletic demonstrations daily in front of the Grandstand. The precision of that detachment was the subject of delighted comment from every side.

So it came about that this five hundred acres of historic ground, on which stood Fort Rouille, upon which a great battle had been fought and where Stanley Barracks, the headquarters of one of the units of Canada's permanent force, still stands, became again a Garrison Reserve echoing and re-echoing to the tramp of marching men, to the stirring music of mili-

100

tary bands, and the blaring of bugles as they marked out the duties for the day.

The C.N.E. and the 2nd World War

By George Kidd

In April, 1942, the decision to give the Canadian Government the facilities at Exhibition Park on a rent free basis, with the government reimbursing the C.N.E. for out-of-pocket expenses, was made. At the conclusion of the war the park and the buildings would be restored to their current condition and returned to the C.N.E.

On May 20, 1942, it was resolved that the Canadian National Exhibition be discontinued for the duration of the war. The motion was carried unanimously and the skeleton staff left on the grounds began to buy Victory Bonds. Nearly everyone else was doing the same thing.

And so the C.N.E. took on a new character. Gone was the smell of hamburgers and onions. Gone, too, was the cry of the barker on the Midway, and the screams of the kids as they tried out one of the rides. And gone were the free samples and the attractive displays.

The buildings became home to thousands of soldiers. They slept in the small stalls in the Horse Palace as they enlisted; the same little stalls that usually contained horses and other animals. The smell of hay and straw were strong but they became pleasant. They slept on double-decker bunks and some of them are still in evidence as you wander through the Horse Palace.

The old Press Building became a dental office and business was good. In the International Building documentation for Military District No. 2 took place, with thousands of men passing in steady file while their life history was typed onto cards and filed away. They would come in with their bright civvie outfits and their long hair. A few hours later the hair and the civvies were gone and all you'd see would be an awkward squad going through the motions in uniforms that never quite fitted.

And so the war continued and the recruits arrived in full force, taking practically every spot in the grounds.

There was only elementary training on the grounds, mostly confined to parades and inspections. Discipline was reasonably strong, but if you were fortunate to get a pass out for a couple of hours and suddenly realized that the TTC would never get you to billets at Lights Out, it was always easy to sneak into the grounds and into your bed.

And the years passed and in 1945, the war ended, General Manager Elwood Hughes had a statement to release to the press.

"Because the military authorities cannot vacate the grounds until May 31, next year, there can be no C.N.E. until 1947."

In his splendid and authoritative book, "Dileas, a History of the 48th Highlanders of Canada," published in 1957, Kim Beattie had much to say about those early days of the war and the C.N.E. But he makes it quite clear that the great love of the boys was the Horse Palace, where their new lives were being shaped.

"The 48th Highlanders were to make themselves at home, as good soldiers always quickly and easily contrive to do, in such a long succession of barracks, billets, tent-lines, hut camps and groups of slit trenches, that many locations on their long war road were to be forgotten," he wrote.

"Not so, the Horse Palace, It was their first war home and the first taste (dubious in the beginning) of barrack and army life for many men. It made a deep impression on individuals. They were to find its memories long remained clear.... The most unhappy memory of the Horse Palace was the choking dust which their steel-caulked boots scraped and stirred from the rough cement floor."

The departure of the soldiers from Exhibition Park was a gigantic one. Although much had been done in preliminary planning for this great exodus, the official date was June 1, 1946.

Trucks moved into the grounds, parking in front of buildings that had been home to so many. Shortly afterwards, loaded with furniture, equipment, books, files and thousands of miscellaneous articles, they moved westward toward the depot's new home at the old Long Branch Small Arms Training School.

Said one newspaper:

"Since 1939 when soldiers were packed into the Horse Palace before going to training centres, countless thousands of troops and air force personnel and the boys of the navy have come to regard the C.N.E. as a place they will long remember.

"Many were sworn in at services there and many of them returned to the same place for their discharge many years after leaving."

The actual move took a full week, and later it was estimated that 12,000 men had lived there and had some minor training; that 23,000 tons of food were consumed as 300,000 men passed through the training camps and went overseas.

Some of the famous units who used the facilities of the C.N.E. during that period were the Toronto Scottish, 48th Highlanders, Royal Regiment, Irish Regiment, Governor General's Foot Guards, South Saskatchewan Regiment, the Black Watch, Lake Superior Regiment, Midland Regiment, Royal Canadian Dragoons, the Royal Canadian Regiment, and others.

The C.N.E. lost five years of its usual history but it was there when the need was felt and it contributed its share to a world at war.

1914 troops – Dufferin Gates

Overland float in Women's Day Parade C.N.E. 1918

Manning Pool entrance, Sentries and service police

H.M.C.S. York February 1942

KNELLER HALL BAND
CANADIAN NATIONAL EXHIBITION.
- 1934 -

Big Bands

... And The Bands Played On

In 1934 an innovation was introduced when the Automotive Building, which had been transformed into a Fashion Show emporium, echoed to the strains of the bands of Abe Lyman, Duke Ellington and Guy Lombardo, as they provided music for those who love gyrations upon an adequate dance floor. In 1935 Rudy Vallee and his Connecticut Yankees visited this building and during their two weeks' stay standing room was at a premium.

The Ballroom, formerly known as the Transportation Building, was for the second year given over wholly to the presentation of feature dance orchestras and to dancing. The engagement of Rudy Vallee with his orchestra and entertainers created widespread interest and the whole production proved immensely popular with the public. The building was transformed by new and attractive lighting and the erection of additional side tiers of seats provided much needed accommodation, particularly while the stage performance was in progress.

While it was anticipated that the public would show great curiosity in the Fleishmann programmes which were broadcast from the building on the two Thursday evenings, there was actually no satisfying the tremendous demand for seats. The novelty of witnessing an important commercial broadcast with

Afternoon concert, Coldstream Guards Band 1903

Bandshell built 1912

many well-known radio performers had an irresistible attraction for large numbers of people. Even after all available space had been utilized for seats, the public still clamoured for tickets and indeed many accepted standing room at a considerable distance from the stage throughout the broadcast.

The following is a list of the Big Bands that have played at the CNE over the years.

1934	1940	1949
Duke Ellington	Duke Ellington	Duke Ellington
Abe Lyman	Jimmy Dorsey	Benny Goodman
Guy Lombardo	Eddie Duchin	Vaughan Monroe
1935	Sammy Kaye	Tommy Dorsey
Rudy Vallee	Tommy Dorsey	Guy Lombardo
1936	Al and Bob Harvey	1950
Rudy Vallee	1941	Guy Lombardo
1937	Tommy Dorsey	Duke Ellington
Horace Heidt	Guy Lombardo	Tommy Dorsey
Guy Lombardo	Ina Ray Hutton	1951
1938	Benny Goodman	Trump Davidson
Benny Goodman	Tony Pastor	Spike Jones (Coliseum)
Guy Lombardo	Vaughn Monroe	More recently:
Tommy Dorsey	The Modernaires	Moxie Whitney
Buddy Rogers	1942-1946	Art Hallman
1939	CNE closed	Mart Kenny &
Glen Gray	during WWII	Norma Locke
Guy Lombardo	1948	Bert Niosi
Benny Goodman	Gene Krupa	
Tony Martin	Tommy Dorsey	
Artie Shaw		
Tommy Dorsey		
Stanley St. John		

Rudy Vallee and his orchestra

Sports

From the Book Fair Sport
by
Bill Leveridge

Mechanical flight was first demonstrated in Toronto during the early days of September, in 1908, when Charles F. Willard, an American aviation pioneer, made exhibition flights at Scarborough Beach. Three attempts to become airborne were made, but on each occasion, soon after take-off, the intrepid pilot and his machine ended up in Lake Ontario. Unsuccessful as it may have been, this was Toronto's first look at an aeroplane in flight.

Six years later, in 1914, the flying boat, "Sunfish," was making daily flights at the Exhibition. Scheduled as Hydro-Aeroplane flights, the craft was powered by an 80 h.p. motor, and was capable of carrying the pilot and two passengers, at speeds of fifty miles an

Left: Gaston Chevrolet races against aviatrix Ruth Law in front of the old C.N.E. grandstand in 1917. The motor car won at this point the aircraft is leading – see top centre of photograph

Right: A descending parachutist touches down after a demonstration jump during the Canadian International Air show

hour on the water, and seventy miles an hour in the air.

The aeroplane soon became involved in sport at the Fair, and in 1917 one of the feature attractions was a race between a low-flying aeroplane, piloted by the American aviatrix, Ruth Law, and an automobile driven by Gaston Chevrolet. The plane had difficulty in making the sharp turns, and the contest was won by the motorcar.

Just two years later, the Canadian National Exhibition sponsored the "Great Toronto-New York Air Race." It was a strange collection of aircraft, including small military training planes and leftover bombers, that entered the competition. The course for this early international race covered a flight from Toronto's Leaside airfield, to New York and return, or from New York to Toronto and return. Contestants were permitted the choice of starting points, and could begin the 1,150 mile flight from either city. The winner was judged by the best flying time taken for the round trip.

Pilots leaving from Toronto, including Lieutenant Duke Schiller, Colonel Billy Barker V.C., and Major "Shorty" Schroeder, received the best wishes of the Prince of Wales, who was present at the take-off. Among those departing from New York were Lieutenant Colonel H. B. Claggett, Lieutenant B. W. Maynard and Major Jack Simmonds. As the course of the race required the pilots to fly across the lake, they equipped themselves with inflated inner tire tubes as a precautionary measure against the risky flight. Lieutenant Colonel Claggett, commissioned by U.S. President Wilson to carry a personal letter to the Prince of Wales, failed to make the delivery, as his machine crashed at Albany, New York. The communication was then given to Lieutenant Maynard, who, unfortunately, lost his way and put down at Windsor. Presumably, the letter arrived by mail.

Major Simmonds met with a harrowing experience when coming in for landing at Leaside. A smoke signal, released to show direction of the wind, fogged the flyer's view. When making the approach to the field, the pilot, flying low over a horse and wagon, caught the wing tip of the aircraft in the harness, and tore it off the frightened animal, without injury to either the horse or to the aeroplane.

A number of aircraft either cracked up or made forced landings along the way. Fortunately, no one was killed.

This historic race was won by Major Rudolph "Shorty" Schroeder, an American, who many years later was the first U.S. pilot to fly a plane in the stratosphere seven miles above earth.

Miss Lillian Boyer, a daring aviatrix, known as the "Empress of the Air," gave daily exhibitions at the waterfront. She was picked up from a speeding motorboat by plane. After becoming sufficiently airborne, the girl made a parachute jump into the lake.

Gordon McCollom, intrepid wing-walker, literally stands on his head to entertain Canadian international airshow crowds

ONTARIO DEPT. OF LANDS & FORESTS

Turbo Beaver during International Air Show 1968

In 1929, aeroplane races from Cleveland to the Exhibition were held.

International seaplane races made their appearance in 1930. The craft flew at very low altitudes over a triangular course of forty-five miles. The start and finish of the event was made on water.

During the years that followed, people were shown the progress which had been accomplished in the air. The huge British dirigible R-100 flew majestically over the grounds. The British Schneider cup plane, Vickers Supermarine Rolls Royce S.6.B., was displayed in the Automotive Building. The Imperial Airway's Flying Boat "Cambria," a pioneer in regular transatlantic service, made a visit and was anchored at the foot of Dufferin Street. In 1939, a young R.C.A.F. pilot, high above the grounds, put the new swift fighter, called the "Hawker Hurricane," through its paces. At that moment few people realized the dramatic role this craft and its successor, the "Spitfire," were to play in the conflict about to come.

After the War, the Ford dirigible made a series of flights at the 1947 Fair, and the R.A.F. "Dambuster" squadron completed the aerial display when sixteen Lincoln bombers gave formation flying demonstrations and other manoeuvres.

All of these exciting events were the forerunners of the spectacular Canadian International Air Show now appearing annually at the waterfront.

AQUARAMA

New horizons for water sports became available in 1934 when a new grandstand and bleacher section was erected at the waterfront. Spectators thronging this area enjoyed the world's best aquatic events, for the price of the general admission to the Exhibition.

About this time, people were experimenting with skis on water, and quite suddenly, with the aid of fast motorboats, a new and exciting sport was born. Water-skiing became a sensation! Young athletes, displaying their skills at aquatic meets, so intrigued the Sports Director, George Duthie, with their ability and daring, that in 1936, he presented a fearless young Dane in the first water-skiing demonstration to be seen at the Fair.

In the year that followed, Captain Douglas Loomis, of Peterborough, Ontario, directed an exhibition of water-skiing and aqua-planing by a group of young Canadians.

Following an exciting water-skiing display in 1939, by Norma, Alex and Russell McIntosh, all young members of a Bobcaygeon, Ontario, family, it became evident to Duthie that Canadians had accepted the sport, and he began to centre his attentions on plans for the future. These plans were, of course, delayed by the events of the 1940's, but at the conclusion of the War, the production of an outstanding waterfront show was uppermost in his mind. He had developed strong contacts with officials of Cypress Gardens, in Florida, and in 1947, Nance Stilley became the first prominent American water-skiing champion to perform at the Exhibition. The show was expanded in 1948, when she was accompanied by Dick Pope, Jr., Buddy Boyle, and members of the Cypress Gardens "Aqua Maids."

American and Canadian skiers combined with all other aquatic sports in the production of an exciting waterfront show. They were the forerunners of the presentation now known as "Aquarama."

Events at the waterfront became bigger and better as the skiing champions from Cypress Gardens continued their thrilling displays. By 1952, the first Canadians, headed by Carol Ann Duthie, were participating in the show, along with athletes from the United States and Mexico. The dazzling display included a water ballet — for the first time, of the drum majorettes, and a parade of nursery rhyme characters, all on water-skis.

Just two years later, a two-hour show named "Watercade" was introduced, and in addition to the acrobatic manoeuvres of the skiers, the production included the agility of the world's champion log-roller, Bill Fontana, of Fort Francis, Ontario, and his dog "Peppy," reputedly the only performing canine log-roller. Up to this time, water-skiing exhibitions

Left to Right: Carol-Ann Duthie (world's junior water ski champion) Arlene Milburn rehearsing for "Aquarama" 1955

had been the mainstay of the waterfront show, but in 1954, national championships were instituted.

Determined that nothing tawdry be associated with his wonderful "Watercade" show, Duthie, in 1955, successfully obtained from "Eaton's of Canada," as a courtesy gesture, settings for the ski numbers. The beautiful costumes for the performers were designed by his wife, and completed by professionals. The show, acclaimed as "superb," achieved international recognition, and was widely publicized by Paramount Pictures and Famous Players Corporation. The spectacle contained hair-raising displays by jumping motorboats, high divers, trampoline artists, comedy clown acts, and prominent water-skiers, including Carol Ann Duthie, Canada's "Queen of the Water Skis."

Climaxing a brilliant career, in which she had won innumerable championships, including world titles, Carol Ann Duthie, Etobicoke's popular water-skier, won the Senior Women's Overall Championship of Canada, for the sixth consecutive year, four as a junior and two as a senior. The feat was accomplished at the Exhibition, after her regular performance in "Watercade," and Carol Ann was chosen "Canada's Outstanding Skier for 1955," Following the victory, the tired but modest young teenager, consented to demonstrate the difficult spin around called "Turn Around Swan." On her first attempt she fell, but not discouraged, and cheered on by a crowd estimated at more than 50,000, the second try was successful, and she became the first Canadian to master the feat. Carol Ann received tremendous ovation,

and was rewarded with superlatives on her physical attributes. Undefeated, she voluntarily ended her career as a competitor; but this talented young Canadian continued as a performer in the waterfront shows, produced and directed by her mother.

The "Watercade" sensation for 1956 was "Lady," a fifteen hundred pound elephant, who gave daily exhibitions on water-skis. The young pachyderm skied sedately inside the sea wall, giving the impression that this was a fine way in which to keep cool and earn a living. The show was further enhanced by the dazzling costumes of the other performers, the beautifully decorated floats and the thrill of high-powered motorboats, zooming up and over the ski ramp.

Spine-tingling novelties became the keynote in 1957 for the extravaganza now called "Aquarama." Bob Maxwell and his high divers, the "Aquazanies," were introduced. A water-ski kite flying act from Florida, and the Bensen flying rowboats and pontoons were added. The show was further augmented by Carol Ann Duthie, riding her lifelike "Snow White Prancing Horses" in breathtaking dashes around the course. "Aquarama" was the final fruition of George Duthie's waterfront dream, and a heartwarming triumph for his family.

Floodlights were installed in 1958, and night performances became possible for "Aquarama." At an evening show in the following year, the area was "invaded" by the crew of the pirate ship "Jose Gasparilla." Armed with swords, muskets, belaying pins and other weapons, the buccaneers stormed the waterfront grandstand, abducted some of the show-

One of the many colourful floats at Aquarama

girls, and made the mock attack quite realistic. In a new feature, a man was handcuffed and roped, put into a sack, and thrown into the water. At each performance, this pseudo "Houdini" made his escape in slightly more than a minute.

A new dimension in publicity was attained in 1960, when Bill Stern, a noted Sports Commentator, had Columbia Pictures film "Aquarama." Used as a sport short, "The Greatest Show on Water" was shown in theatres throughout the world.

Johnnie Rivers and his high diving mules, were added to the 1962 show, and brought gales of laughter to the waterfront. The late Charlie Godfrey, the physiotherapist for aquatic sports, related a story of his small dog, who had taken an intense dislike to one particular mule. As a result, the stable area was full of their yapping and braying. One day the mule was quietly waiting his turn to perform when Charlie and his dog arrived. Without warning, the ferocious tyke rushed the unsuspecting mule, and sharply nipped its heels. Completely surprised, the mule bolted, with the dog in hot pursuit, and much to the delight of the spectators, made a hurried and unscheduled dive into the lake. Charlie jokingly said, "I was not surprised when officials cancelled my dog's admission pass." In this same year, the world's champion kite flyer, Ken Tibado and his partner, did death defying acrobatics high up in the sky.

In 1972, "Aquarama" was produced by Outboard Marine Corporation of Canada, and directed by Jack Perdue, of Peterborough. It was an all Canadian, professional show, combining suspense, beauty, and laughter.

Accidents were rare in this strenuous show, but minor injuries were sustained by Billy Jean Clarke, who lost some teeth in a kite flying mishap, and by David Armstrong, who suffered a whiplash in a pre-show ski-jumping contest.

New novelties made their appearance at the waterfront in 1973, and again in 1974. During this time, "Aquarama" was produced by Life Savers Ltd., the "candy" people. The extravaganza highlighted the "Dancing Boat," whose driver literally stood the craft on end and pirouetted sprightly over the waves; the "Hovercraft," demonstrating a machine that may well revolutionize the known ways of transportation; an Aquamaid's daring routines on the "Flying Wing"; a 100 m.p.h. racing boat; the "Gyrocopter," a hand powered air vehicle, doing a series of remarkable gyrations; a "Fashion Show" on skis, and the famed "Flying Circus." Added to all of these, were soaring kites, trick ski performers, clowns, and the ballet routines by the Aquamaids.

"Aquarama" '75, the thrill packed and humorous watershow that was the pride of the C.N.E. and the envy of all other north American exhibitions, remained under the direction of Jack Perdue. Among the twenty-three Canadian performers were the smiling, talented Clark sisters from Orillia, Ontario.

On Sunday, August 24th, more than four thousand onlookers were stunned, as kite flier, Daniel Genge of Toronto, fell five hundred feet into Lake Ontario. The wings of his kite had collapsed under the strain of strong, gusty winds, and he barely missed landing on the concrete breakwater. Unable to free himself from the debris, the young man was rescued by members of the "Aquarama" team, whose quick action prevented the situation from becoming more serious. The flier was rushed to St. Joseph's Hospital, and happily made a quick recovery from injuries that might have ended with dire consequences.

Rothman's Aquarama was produced and directed in 1977 by Dave Sutherland, and co-ordinated by Beverly Clark. The exciting aquatic extravaganza was superbly executed by a crew, fondly described by Sutherland, "as the finest young people I have known."

The show moved rapidly from act to act, one with a brilliant performance of barefoot skiing by Greg McEvoy, of Port Colborne, that covered two lengths of the course, and another, a twelve-tier skiing pyramid, which introduced two newcomers, the 18-year-old identical twins, Lori and Lynn Herod of Etobicoke. The laughs and amusement were provided by Peter O'Mara, "Fuzz" Woolner, and Greg McEvoy, in numerous comical antics, and a waterlogged specialty of the "Blue Jays" trying for a home run.

The forty-five minute performance ended with a breathtaking flight by Paul Roberts, of Stratford, who cruised his colourful hand glider at one thousand feet and gracefully guided the frail craft in a free fall landing at the Aquarama site.

Kite flyer Jerry Blaggett coming in for a landing

Acquarama – early comedy team

Auto Polo 1913

Johnny Rainey, champion light car driver of the world

AUTO SPORTS

Automobiles appeared in a sports event at the grandstand for the first time in 1913, and before a capacity crowd, the hair-raising capabilities of the vehicle were displayed, in the form of auto-polo. For this game, the cars were stripped to the chassis, leaving two seats over the gasoline tank, one for the driver, and the other for the mallet man. The driver skilfully twisted and turned the car, sometimes up-side down, as he endeavoured to get close enough to the ball, for the mallet man, standing on the running board, to hit it toward the opponent's goal. It was a tremendously exciting sport. The program was even made more spectacular in the following year, by the addition of periodical races and hurdling in motor-cars. It was during 1919 that the popular speed king, Ralph De Palma, was invited to drive the world's fastest car in a test against time on the track. Speeds at that time had not reached one hundred miles per hour.

To greet the "Roaring Twenties," the Exhibition instituted official auto races, with an added marathon event in 1920. The prizes offered amounted to $9,000. Present day promoters would look down their noses at this attempt to break records on a half-mile track with sharp turns, but at least the drivers, the public, and the officials, revelled in the noise, the reek of

gasoline fumes, the clouds of dust and the over-powering excitement of competition. No world records were shattered, but the races were successful for several years. In the autumn of 1928, the meet had outgrown the available facilities, and after the Fair closed in that year, automobile racing was abandoned.

Just two years later, the new and impressive Automotive Building, at the eastern end of the grounds, was opened to the public. Primarily intended for the display of passenger cars, the building, on occasion, exhibited cars used by world celebrated racing drivers. The first of these was an example of British engineering and design, in a magnificent personal car owned and driven by speedster, Don Kaye. This was followed in 1936 by a display of the world's fastest motorcar, "The Blue-bird," which had been driven on the salt flats of Utah by Sir Malcolm Campbell of England, at the tremendous speed of 304.331 miles per hour. This daring driver visited the Exhibition for the time that this famous car was on display. The history of man's attacks on the one mile speed record in an automobile, dates back to the year 1898, when the Frenchman, Chasseloup-Laubat, amazed the world by driving a car over a measured mile, at the astonishing rate of thirty-nine miles an hour.

BICYCLE RACING

Cycle racing came to the Fair in 1880, and with few exceptions, the sport provided annual competitions lasting until 1970. This was a distinction paralleled by only one other sport to be seen at the Exhibition.

The bicycle, once termed "a nuisance and a menace on the road," was a new kind of transport that could labour without hay and oats, storage was simple, and there was no stable to clean. Furthermore, the machine moved people with relative ease and at little cost. These were simple, economic facts not to be ignored.

People scoffed at the possibility of locomotion, by means of a chain running on a toothed wheel, but a ride on the new-fangled machine soon changed their minds. The bicycle was a success! Soon, cycling clubs were formed, and by 1896, it was reported there were more than 200,000 cyclists in Canada.

For several years, a moderate program of racing appeared at the grandstand track, and with the bicycle gaining in public favour, new innovations were sought. By 1888, the machines were matched against horses. It was also decided to hold a championship match between Miss Jessie Oakes, of England, and Miss Elsie Von Blumen, champion lady cyclist of the United States. This distinguished international competition was presented each day, and the final deciding heats were contested on the last Friday.

Racing continued for some time on the chain-drive, safety bicycles, first designed in 1873, by a man named H. J. Lawson, of Brighton, England. These machines were mostly equipped with pneumatic tires, which were the brainchild of an Irish Veterinarian named John Boyd Dunlop, who developed them in late 1887. Originally fashioned from a piece of garden hose, the tire was inflated with water, until a friend of Boyd's suggested blowing up the tire with air. As a result of this suggestion, the first pneumatic tires were fitted to the rear wheels of a tricycle, and were used successfully in February, 1888.

Sometime during 1894, the Dunlop Rubber Company presented a Challenge Cup for competition among Ontario cyclists. This resulted in exciting twenty mile events, that were sometimes raced on machines equipped with solid rubber tires, considered to be more reliable than the puncture-prone pneumatic type. Competitions for the Dunlop Cup and other trophies, were completely dominated by riders from the Royal Canadian Cycle Club. In nine successive years of racing, until 1902, this famous club won the Dunlop trophy on eight occasions, and it became their permanent property. This emblem of cycling supremacy is prominently displayed at the Royal Canadian Curling Club in Toronto.

Open, handicap, and invitation races, over distances one mile, three miles, and five miles, became standard competitions, and in 1911 an entry fee of twenty-five cents was first instituted. Sport was dormant at the Fair during the time of the first World War, but soon returned after the close of hostilities.

Track champions made their appearance, and in the postwar years, they created a sensation in matched races held over various distances. These events were commonly decided by the best two-out-of-three heats, and the grandstand track became a hub of cycling activity.

Soon, national and international championships were organized, involving the leading track stars from Canada and the United States. In 1933, the world's leading Six-Day bicycle riders competed in a special fifty-mile team race.

By the end of the decade, the Ontario bicycle championships brought enthusiastic competition to the meet. Those pleasant conditions came to a halt during a part of 1940, while nations sought to settle their differences on a much different field.

Starting line for bicycle races!

117

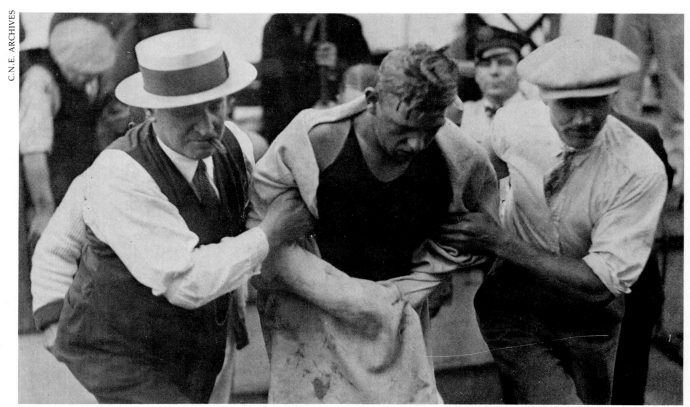

George Young who won the first Wrigley Marathon swim in California in January 1927 was responsible for the introduction of the most popular sporting event ever held at the C.N.E.

MARATHON SWIMS

George Young was the man really responsible for the introduction of Marathon Swims and the public acceptance of sport at the Canadian National Exhibition.

In the fall of 1926, it became known that a Marathon Swim was planned over a course between the mainland of California and Santa Catalina Island, a distance of about twenty miles. William Wrigley, Junior, of Chicago, had offered a prize of $25,000 to the swimmer finishing first.

George, then a 17-year- old boy, had gained considerable recognition in Toronto swimming circles under the tutelage of coach Johnnie Walker, and became intrigued with the opportunity of entering the Catalina Marathon.

Inspired by the possibility of winning this fabulous prize, which would bring financial stability to his hard-working mother, George took off for California, accompanied by his friend, Bill Hastings. The journey was started on an antiquated motorcycle. Disaster struck in the State of Arkansas when the machine completely broke down. But the fates were kind. The two boys were given a lift by a young couple driving to Los Angeles. Safely lodged in that city, with a family friend named Henry Doc O'Bryne, George immediately started serious training for the swim.

Entries in the Catalina Marathon numbered about one hundred of the best long-distance swimmers in the world. The unknown boy from Toronto was conceded little or no chance of being a serious contender.

The final result was typical of making predictions on the outcome of any sport. George Young won the Catalina Swim. On January 16, 1927, screaming headlines in the newspapers of Canada, the United States, and other countries of the world, blared the news. Overcoming the finest competitors swimming had to offer, and the ordeal of being buffeted by rough, salty seas, cold water, the vagaries of changing tides, the unpleasantness of clinging kelp, and shaking off the attention of an inquisitive shark, he had accomplished the impossible. The only swimmer to finish the course, covering about thirty miles in 15 hours 46 minutes, he was accorded a tremendous ovation.

George became his home-town idol. Upon his return to Toronto, he was given a hero's welcome. Although he had been presented with a house, through popular subscription, any vision of riches was quickly dissipated. His mother had signed an agreement with Doc O'Bryne, giving him forty per cent on all George's winnings. Financial agreements and management remained a serious problem with George throughout his career.

Officials of the C.N.E., assisted by William Wrigley, Jr., realized that George was the best individual attraction in their history. A Marathon Swim was arranged for the 1927 Fair. The swim and the entry of George Young became the special feature of the year.

The publicity of the Catalina Swim had aroused public interest to such a pitch, that the 1927 C.N.E. Marathon Swim resulted in record attendance at the Fair.

At the opening of the 1927 Exhibition, a feeling of excitement and anticipation prevailed. A new and ambitious program was about to be embarked upon, which for a time, was to make the C.N.E. the professional and amateur swimming centre of the world. The staging of the Marathon Swim, for a purse of $50,000 arranged by the Exhibition in conjunction with the William Wrigley Company of Canada, offered the greatest sporting event in aquatic history.

The Marathon was scheduled to start on the morning of August 31, at 8:30 a.m. One hundred and seventy-four swimmers and natatorial champions, representing thirty nationalities, had entered this open event. They would gather at the starting point at 8:00 a.m., to receive full instructions for the world's greatest swimming event.

It was a beautiful, cloudless morning, and a large crowd had gathered at the waterfront. Now, regardless of any previous arrangements that had been made concerning acceptable water temperatures before the race would be allowed to start, it could hardly be a factor at this favourable moment. The contestants were on the barges, the weather was clear, the lake was not rough, and the attendance kept rapidly building. Obviously, to C.N.E. officials, the stage was set. The official approval was given. The swimmers applied liberal amounts of grease to their bodies. Then, facing the starting line, as the gun was fired, they took the plunge — THE SWIM WAS ON!

Immediately following the plunge, a near tragedy occurred. None of the contestants had been screened for their swimming ability. Lured by the possibility of winning fame and fortune, some entrants could hardly swim at all. Early on the morning of the Swim, a young man pleaded to become a contestant. Accepting his story, the officials allowed him to enter. Quickly he prepared himself, and then applied very black grease to his body. Now ready to start, as the gun was fired, he jumped into the water — straight to the bottom. Realizing the danger, Charlie Godfrey, an official of the Marathon, resplendent in a white suit, dived in and quickly had the gasping man's head out of the water. Both men were safely landed on the starting barge. Charlie ruefully inspected his suit, now well smeared with black grease. Brusquely, he addressed the wet young man, "You can't swim, why are you here?" Came the sheepish reply, "I had bet $25 I could enter the swim and came from Kirkland Lake to prove it."

The course was in the form of a triangle. The contestants would start at the eastern end of the C.N.E. waterfront, directly south of the Princes' Gates, and swim one mile west inside the protection of the sea wall. At this point, they would enter the lake through

Wrigley Marathon Boat

PUBLIC ARCHIVES OF CANADA

Start of the 1929 race

119

Greased and ready to go

"Pigskin Peters" (alias Hap Watson), popular Toronto Star columnist, shakes hands with J. Allan Ross, Canadian head of the William Wrigley Jr. Company Limited, sponsores of the first three C.N.E. marathon swims.

a sea wall gap and swim three miles to a buoy marking the apex of the triangle, and would then swim three miles to the starting point, completing seven miles. They were required to cover the course three times around, a distance of twenty-one miles.

The swimmers had been instructed to locate their boats and attendants at the end of the first mile. Too late, it was realized, this was to cause endless confusion. The official boats were grouped together near the gap. Many of the swimmers arrived simultaneously at this point, and it was almost impossible for the men in the boats to locate their respective charges, but, by diligent search, this was partially accomplished. Many contestants had already been taken from the water. Others, not wanting to lose valuable time, had passed through the gap and were headed for the buoy anchored three miles out in the lake. They were without guidance or protection and vulnerable to disaster. The jumble was gradually sorted out; the swimmers found boats and proceeded under adequate protection.

Officials of the C.N.E. were responsible for the safety regulations. Each contestant supplied a boat, which carried his coach or trainer, an oarsman and a C.N.E. observer. Large motorboats and cruisers ranged the course and could respond quickly to any point where danger threatened. Volunteer officials were placed at strategic points and the assistance they rendered to cold and exhausted swimmers was superb. A C.N.E. hospital tent, with doctors and nurses in attendance, was also provided to give adequate medical attention. The Toronto Harbour Commission was responsible for policing the course.

Earlier in the morning, and for the purpose of checking the water temperature, Elwood Hughes, C.N.E. Sports Director, and Hap Watson, went to the sea wall. Hap lifted the thermometer from the water and said to Elwood, "What was that acceptable water temperature again, 56°?" Elwood replied, "Yes, that's the lowest." In relating this story Hap said, "I looked at this instrument and read 44° when I took it out of the water, but by holding it in my hand I finally got it up to 66° before handing it to Elwood. But I was actually startled, because don't forget, as 'Pigskin,' I had to swim that firs mile."

Five minutes after the official start, Hap Watson, in the guise of "Pigskin Peters," a comic character he portrayed for the Toronto Star, plunged into the water and supplied relief to the drama being enacted in the first mile of the swim. Fully clothed, wearing a bowler hat and knee high rubber boots, Hap scrambled through the first mile of his ordeal with the aid of fifteen feet of piano wire fastened to a boat on one end and to a belt on his person at the other. (An excellent swimmer, the wire provided Hap with protection in the event the weight of his clothing became a hazard). Hap related this experience with great relish, but added, "The cold of the water was unbelievable." His act completed, with the famous bowler hat dripping icicles, he was taken from the water, his body was blue from cold, and his teeth chattering. Arriving at the C.N.E. hospital, immediate help arrived in the form of whiskey. Being a non-drinker, Hap was not able to down this fiery stimulant, and most of it was spilled over him. Reluctant to waste the whiskey, the attendants proceeded to rub the liquor into Hap's body in an effort to get it inside him. As soon as he was warm and properly dressed, Hap took up his prearranged post as an official at the buoy three miles out in the lake.

From early morning thousands of excited people had thronged through the Exhibition gates. The largest crowd to watch a sports event in Canada, or possibly, in the world, had jammed the waterfront. The name of George Young was on every lip. All were sure he would finish first, and not a person present had even the slightest doubt but that he would outclass all others and win in record time.

But what of George Young, the home-town idol? His Catalina accomplishment had made the prospect of an easy victory in the marathon a subject of widespread publicity during the preceding weeks. Carefully trained by his coach, Johnnie Walker, George was in excellent physical condition for the race. But Walker was to say later, "Long before the race, George was in a constant state of anxiety; the boy knew he was expected to win and realized he needed to be at his very best." At the start of the race, George settled into his wonderful stride and made good progress. But as time passed by, it became evident he was in trouble. Weighed down by the knowledge he was expected to win with ease, his sense of responsibility to Toronto and his followers had him ill-prepared mentally and emotionally for the ordeal. The dreadful cold of the water seeped into his youthful frame, and his resistance steadily diminished. Half frozen, and dreadfully tired after swimming five-and-a-half miles, he suddenly stopped and asked to be taken from the water.

Attention was now focused on Ernst Vierkoetter, who was swimming strongly through the icy water and had gained a commanding lead. By mid-afternoon, only three swimmers remained in the race, Vierkoetter of Germany, Michel of France; and Erickson of the United States.

Ernst Vierkoetter won the race! Finishing the twenty-one mile course in 11 hours 45 minutes, he was remarkably fresh and waved happily to the wildly cheering throng gathered near the finishing barge. The handsome Wrigley Trophy, emblematic of the Marathon Swimming Championship of the World, along with $30,000, was the reward Ernst Vierkoetter received for his remarkable feat in conquering the icy waters of Lake Ontario.

The C.N.E. Marathon was an endurance contest rather than a race. The finest swimmers of the era had entered the swim and all but three had succumbed to the dreadful cold of the water. From an outstanding entry of female swimmers, none became a serious contender in the race.

The first C.N.E. — Wrigley Marathon Swim was ended. Foster Hewitt had made the first radio broadcast of a professional swim in Canada. Ernst Vierkoetter was crowned Champion of the World. The Exhibition had benefited by unprecedented national and international publicity and by the largest attendance of its history. C.N.E. officials later reported that "the attendance record of 1,870,000 persons entering the gates in two weeks, eclipsed the 1926 record by 297,000, truly a remarkable showing." The Sports Department had definitely established its position with the Fair. But regardless of these happenings, or the changes in rules or format to improve conditions of the swim, the spectre of bitterly cold waters would always remain.

The third marathon, held in 1928, was divided into a women's section, over a distance of ten miles, and a men's section, over a distance of fifteen miles. Prize money was allocated proportionately for the two events, which were scheduled for different days. This was to remain the pattern, with modifications as to distance and prize monies, for marathon swims at the Exhibition for a great many years.

The women's race in the third marathon, over a distance of ten miles, was won by Ethel Hertle, of New York, on August 29. She was awarded the trophy and top prize. The men's race, at fifteen miles, was held on September 5. Not one of the 199 entrants in this event succeeded in finishing, on account of the very cold water. Division of the total prize money was made to the fourteen swimmers who made the best showing. Each received $2,500.

The "Big Swims," for the World's Professional Championship, remained an attraction until 1937. The best national and international swimmers continued to compete. The excitement and drama of the events, the hopes and disappointments of the contestants, were always present, and Lake Ontario continued its threat of cold water conditions.

Women Finishing First

1927 No woman finished this open event of approximately 21 miles

1928 Ethel Hertle, Bronx, N.Y.
Distance 10 miles

1929 Martha Norelius, New York City
Distance 10 miles

1930 Margaret Ravior, Philadelphia
Distance 10 miles

1931 Margaret Ravior, Philadelphia
Distance 10 miles

1932 Margaret Ravior, Philadelphia
Distance 10 miles

1933 Ruth Tower Corsan, Toronto
Distance 10 miles

1934 May Looney, Warren, Ohio
Distance 5 miles

1935 Charlotte Acres, Vancouver, B.C.
Distance 5 miles

1936 Susan Robertson, Sea Bright, N.J.
Distance 3 miles

1937 Lenore Wingard, Homestead, PA
Distance 3 miles

1947 Bernice Looney, Warren, Ohio
Distance 5 miles

1948 Bernice Looney, Warren, Ohio
Distance 5 miles

1949 Bernice Looney, Warren, Ohio
Distance 5 miles

1950 Bernice Looney, Warren, Ohio
Distance 3 miles

1951 Vivian King, Winnipeg, Manitoba
Distance 3 miles

1952 Shirley Campbell, Fergus, Ontario
Distance 3 miles

1953 Shirley Campbell, Fergus, Ontario
Distance 3 miles

Men Finishing First

1927 Ernst Vierkoetter, Cologne, Germany
Distance 21 miles

1928 Not one of the entrants finished the course due to extremely cold water
Distance 15 miles

1929 Ed Keating, New York City
Distance 15 miles

1930 Marvin Nelson, Fort Dodge, Iowa
Distance 15 miles

1931 George Young, Toronto, Ontario
Distance 15 miles

1932 George Blagden, Memphis, Tennessee
Distance 15 miles

1933 Marvin Nelson, Fort Dodge, Iowa
Distance 15 miles

1934 Marvin Nelson, Fort Dodge, Iowa
Distance 15 miles

1935 Gianni Gambi, Ravena, Italy
Distance 15 miles

1936 Frank Pritchard, Buffalo, New York
Distance 5 miles

1937 Frank Pritchard, Buffalo, New York
Distance 5 miles

1947 Ben Gazel, Toronto, Ontario
Distance 10 miles

1948 Stephen Wozniak, Buffalo, New York
Distance 10 miles

1949 Cliff Lumsdon, New Toronto, Ontario
Distance 15 miles

1950 Cliff Lumsdon, New Toronto, Ontario
Distance 15 miles

Ethel Hertle of New York won ten mile race

Start of the 1935 Women's Marathon Swim. Note how the women have streamlined their costumes.

1951   Jerry Kerschner, Columbus, Ohio
        Distance 10 miles

1952   Cliff Lumsdon, New Toronto, Ontario
        Distance 10 miles

1953   Cliff Lumsdon, New Toronto, Ontario
        Distance 10 miles

1954   Canadian Marathon Team
        Distance 30 miles
        Cliff Lumsdon:
        Tom Park:
        Ben Gazel:
        George Bevan:

1955   Cliff Lumsdon, New Toronto, Ontario
        Distance 32 miles

1961   Herman Willemse, Holland
        Distance 15 miles

1962   Herman Willemse, Holland
        Distance 15 miles

1963   Abdel Abou Heif, Egypt
        Distance 15 miles

1964   Not one of the entrants finished
        the course due to adverse weather conditions
        Distance 32 miles

MOTORBOATS

Motorboat races were first scheduled at the Exhibition in 1910. Three races were held daily from September 3 to September 8, and these classes competed.

Class 'A' — Free-for-all over triangular course.
Class 'B' — Free-for-all straight away mile trials.
Class 'C' — Handicap — Boats of speed under 25 miles an hour and over 18 miles.
Class 'D' — Handicap — Boats over 12 miles an hour and up to and including 15 miles.
Class 'F' — Handicap — Boats over 9 miles an hour and up to and including 12 miles.
Class 'G' Handicap — All boats up to and including 9 miles.

Insignificant as these speeds may seem, boatmen of the era who had previously struggled with cumbrous oars, often on turbulent waters, thrilled at the mobility of the power driven craft.

At this time, no one had the vaguest notion that in less than fifty years, Donald Campbell, a young Englishman, would establish a speed record of 225 m.p.h. on water. On the first run, he hurled his jet-propelled hydroplane, "Bluebird," through the water at the incredible speed of 287.78 m.p.h. The feat was accomplished at Coniston Water, England, in September 1956.

The sport flourished, and American boatmen, who lauded the Exhibition course as one of the best on the continent, added international rivalry to this rapidly expanding activity. As time passed, "mile-a-minute" motorboats from the United States sped along the waterfront.

The Exhibition facility became the official course of the Toronto Motorboat Club, the International Powerboat Union, and the American Powerboat Association in 1920. In that year, six days of racing were held for a variety of displacement boats, which culminated with the Great Lakes International $1,000 Gold Cup, a free-for-all scratch race of thirty miles.

Harry Greening, of Hamilton, showed a tremendous interest in the development of powerboat racing. In the words of Harry "Red" Foster, a boating buff himself, "Greening was the father of Canadian motorboating." Greening, who was seen at the waterfront on frequent occasions, associated himself with Herb Ditchburn, of Gravenhurst. Together, they developed fast powerboats that brought Greening into competition in the prestigious Gold Cup races on the Detroit River.

Gradually, the power plants and displacement of the boats was increased, and speed became a byword.

Toward the close of the decade, the roar in the "Roaring Twenties" was enhanced by the development of a new phenomenon — outboard motors —

an innovation that brought powered mobility to many types of watercraft. Given prominence by the vigorous enthusiasm of Lou Marsh, this new source of power was attached to a flimsy contraption, called the "Sea Flea," which was soon hurtling across the water at amazing speeds.

The inimitable "Red" Foster was the winner of the first "Sea Flea" race, held at the Fair in 1929. The event provoked an interest that prevailed at the waterfront for many years.

The visit by the Irish born "speed king," Kaye Don, caused a welter of excitement at the C.N.E. in 1931. It had been arranged that at the conclusion of the Harmsworth Trophy race on the Detroit River, he would appear at the Fair with his craft, Miss England II. Unfortunately, Don was duped into losing the "Harmsworth" by an American, Gar Wood, which resulted in a storm of controversy. Soon after this unhappy experience, Don arrived at Toronto with a damaged Miss England II, and was extended a welcome in keeping with his achievements. Later in October, the sponsor of this enterprise, Lord Wakefield, sent a letter of appreciation to the Exhibition for the many kindnesses extended Kaye Don, and wrote, "I am sorry that circumstances made it impossible for him to make a further attempt upon the World's Water Speed Record in Canadian waters, but I am glad to think that the exhibition of the boat, at your magnificent Canadian National Exhibition, was of some assistance to that great effort."

After being eclipsed for a time by the "Sea Fleas," in the mid-thirties the more powerful inboards regained some of their former popularity. In 1934, the useful 225 cubic inch class engaged in an International Powerboat Race over a distance of fifteen miles, acclaimed by the C.N.E. as the "Championship of the World." The event, which attracted ten starters, including six from the United States, was won by Harold Wilson, of Ingersoll, Ontario, driving "Little Miss Canada Third." The local driver, "Red" Foster, was runner-up on points for the championship, although his craft, "The Atom," konked out. In 1935, Wilson repeated his win with "Little Miss Canada Fourth," but was later dethroned by Gordon Adamson, of Highland Park, Illinois. In 1940, the championship was gained by the world's record holder, "Pops" Cooper, of Kansas City. The American drivers in the race praised the efficient arrangements made for the regatta, and lauded the help given by the Toronto Harbour Commission and the Toronto Lifesaving Service. The "Sea Fleas" also appeared, and the Canadian Championships for classes "A," "B," and "C" were all taken by a young Quebec airman, Mel Smith. A new amateur speed record of 49.1 m.p.h was set by Leon Guthrie, of Cleveland. Another American made a professional record by forcing his craft over a measured mile in 59 seconds.

At the request of the Fuel Controller, all racing was cancelled at the Fair in 1941. In a spirit of goodwill, American sportsmen offered gasoline and oil to be used, free of charge, by Canadian drivers at the Exhibition. On instructions from the Fuel Control Board, this generous offer was declined.

Motorboat racing was resumed in 1947. The boats of many drivers who had promised to compete at the Fair, had been damaged in rough water at prior regattas, and they were unable to keep their commitment. "Miss Canada" was among these damaged craft, but her owner, Harold Wilson, allowed his son to drive the boat inside the sea wall. This demonstration convinced a huge throng that the boat would one day succeed in winning the coveted Gold Cup.

During the last year, a tribute was paid to the memory of two outstanding American boatmen — Eddie Mattas and "Pops" Cooper — who had recently lost their lives in racing accidents. Both had raced at the Exhibition on numerous occasions.

Throughout the 1950's, there was a great proliferation of aquatic events, and the waterfront blossomed as the core of the sports program. Motorboating had become a viable sport, and the diverse competitions attracted outstanding drivers with every conceivable type of power driven craft. The continual roar of powerful motors had a magnetic fascination for the public, and large numbers watched the races.

In the early years of this decade, drivers raced inboards, outboards, and hydroplanes, for varying cash prizes, silverware, and other trophies. In 1952, the boatmen and officials mourned the passing of Frank Smith, an enthusiastic competitor, who died during the course of boating events. Two years later, Keith Cavanagh, of Perth, and Bob Glenny, from Dunnville, emerged double-heat winners in the various classes.

After his speedboat had crashed the sea wall on the opening day of the races, Jim Walker, of Oshawa, was taken from the water unconscious. The hospital confirmed that Walker had a broken wrist and concussion.

Bill Hodgson – Argonaut football team owner set many records at the C.N.E. during the mid-1950's

In the championship races, held in 1956, the Toronto racing enthusiast, Bill Hodgson, piloted his record-breaking hydroplane, "Miss O'Keefe," at a new speed of 103.5 m.p.h. for the waterfront course. This intrepid driver had previously set a world mark of 125.8 m.p.h. with his craft at Picton, Ontario.

A crowd of 50,000 reportedly gathered at the waterfront in 1957, to watch the British speed king, Donald Campbell, drive his jet-propelled hydroplane "Bluebird," along the racing course. In this demonstration, the world's fastest boat grazed the sea wall at a speed of 130 m.p.h., but received only minor damage. It is recorded that developments which Campbell had incorporated in "Bluebird" were patented, and were so significant that many of them were put on the secret list by the British Admiralty.

During his stay at the Fair, the famous driver's trophies were on display, and he, himself, was available at the "Bluebird" exhibit to answer random questions asked by the public.

A decade of motorboat activity was climaxed with fantastic tricks, demonstrated by a flotilla of flight-jumping boats, powered by outboard motors. These craft were a spectacular addition to the 1959 stock outboard races.

The world famous Canadian speedboat, "Miss Supertest III," entered the Sports Hall of Fame in 1960. Owned by Jim Thompson, of London, and driven by Canadian Bob Hayward, the propeller-driven craft, powered by an enormous 2000 h.p. Rolls Royce engine, had won the ardently sought Harmsworth trophy in the previous year. The boat successfully defended her title on Canadian waters in 1960 and 1961, and was retired in 1962, after Hayward's fatal accident of September 10, 1961. "Miss Supertest III" appeared on display at the Exhibition, and was also exhibited on occasion at the Sportsmen's Show.

The early years of 1960 saw much stock hydroplane racing, and drivers enjoyed the championship races that were operated in conjunction with the Canadian Boating Federation.

These were gala years for the boatmen, and in 1967, the "Centennial" regatta opened with a colourful decorated Boat Parade. This was followed by a two hour International Powerboat Marathon for sportscraft with stock production engines. Choppy water proved hazardous in this event, and a rash of accidents prevented many drivers from finishing. A driver from Ypsilanti saw his boat sink after being damaged by rough water. Later, another American boat suffered serious damage. Both craft were salvaged by the rescue crew. And so it went, with only thirty-five of the seventy-one starting boats finishing the course, described as rough and treacherous. John Pietra, of Louisville, Kentucky, was the winner of this ordeal. He completed twenty-three 4-mile laps in 1 hour 56 ½ minutes. At a dinner following the race, $8,600 was awarded in prizes. Accidents remained a serious problem in the outboard races that followed,

and the driving skill of John Webster, of Scarborough, gained him a dramatic victory. Until 1970, Webster drove roughshod over his competitors, and regardless of water conditions, finished first in one or more classes for outboards.

In 1972, Toronto drivers took eight of the nine classes to dominate competition for the Belvedere Challenge Cup. Among the forty competitors in this sportscraft event, the lone victory of Andre Savard, of Lucerne, Quebec prevented a clean sweep by local boatmen.

Regattas for motorboats, large and small, had been on the sports program almost continuously since 1910. Major championships had been taken elsewhere, and the noisy competitions no longer fascinated visitors at the Fair.

With a view to entertaining those who thrive on speed and noise, in 1974, a number of daring young men and their flat-bottomed 427 cubic inch high-speed inboard craft, were brought to the Fair in a series of thrilling Drag Boat races that pre-empted all other motorboat activity at the waterfront. From a standing start, Dick Buller, of Niagara Falls, hurled his craft over the quarter mile course in 9.50 seconds, taking top prize of $1,000 and the trophy by Life Saver Company.

Twelve boats competed in the Drag Boat races in 1975. Speeding at 110 m.p.h., Gary McLauran, Ottawa, drove for an average time of 9.38 seconds in the two-day meet, over the quarter-mile course, to win the purse and trophy donated by Peter Stuyvesant 100's. His closest competitor, Dick Buller, averaged 10.20 seconds.

A highlight of 1976, was the appearance of Mrs. Linda Lewis, of Kenmore, New York, the first lady driver to enter the Drag Boat races at the waterfront. A former "Miss Buffalo" in 1971, and now a homemaker with an eight-month-old daughter, Mrs. Lewis failed to qualify for the final heats, but did attain speeds of 95 m.p.h. over the course.

During a qualifying run at the start of the finals, Maurice Claveau, of St. Jean Baptiste, Quebec, was thrown from his craft as it over-turned at a speed in excess of 100 m.p.h. He was hospitalized with a fractured arm and rib injuries.

Cyril Smith, of Orillia, won the overall championship, the trophy and prize money of $1,000, by narrowly defeating Norman Phillips, of Bowmanville, who placed second. Other Canadians, Brian Butson and Dick Buller, finished third and fourth respectively, to beat nine American drivers in the clamorous but exciting competition.

The tremendous roar of the 575 h.p. engines during the two-day Drag Boat races in 1977, attracted many people to the waterfront. Surviving the elimination races, a local boatman, Mel Trovochka, of Mississauga, went on to win the championship and $1,000. Terry Foahs, of Jacksonville, Florida, placed second, gathering $500 in prize money.

The world famous oarsman Jake Gaudaur of Orillia, who won the matched sculling race at the First Exhibition in 1879

rowing

Since the late 1850's, Toronto has spawned a number of oarsmen, who have brought fame to Canada. The first was Ned Hanlan. Born at Toronto Island in 1855, he developed his natural aptitude by rowing a skiff a mile-and-a-half each day to and from school. He entered competition in 1871, and by 1880, became the first Canadian to capture the sculling championship of the world.

Another Canadian, Jake Gaudaur, 18, a native of Orillia, commenced his competitive career in 1876 at Barrie. Here he finished second to Hanlan and Riley, who had finished first in a dead heat. Three years later, in 1879, at the first Exhibition, Gaudaur won a matched race and a purse of $300, against a local oarsman named McKen. In a career that covered twenty-five years, Gaudaur captured many of the championships that sculling had to offer, and in 1896, at age 38, he became the second Canadian to win the coveted championship of the world. Over the years,

the competitive rivalry between Gaudaur and Hanlan was intense, each managing to defeat the other from time to time. An illustrious son of the famous Gaudaur reports that his sire won over Hanlan on twelve different occasions.

The names of Ned Hanlan and Jake Gaudaur are enshrined in the hallowed halls of Canada's Sports Hall of Fame. In addition to this honour, a bronze statue, commemorating Ned Hanlan, who had died in 1908, was unveiled at the Exhibition in 1926. Standing on a granite pedestal in his racing togs, holding a pair of oars and looking toward his former Island home, the likeness of this famous oarsman is an inspiring sight. It is not generally known that Joe Wright, Jr., another eminent Toronto sculler, posed for this sculpture.

Competitive rowing was first instituted at the Exhibition in 1923, in a match race between the Leander Club of England, Undine Club of Philadelphia, and the Argonaut Club of Toronto. The race was won by the Leander Club.

C.N.E. grounds unveiling of Hanlan Memorial 1926, Mrs. Hanlan pictured left first row

From that time forward, rowing appeared regularly on the sports program, in events that included lightweight and heavyweight singles, lightweight and heavyweight fours with coxswain, and 135 lb., 145 lb., 155 lb., and heavyweight eights. The events of various distances were open to amateurs.

In the days of the roaring twenties, Joe Wright and Jack Guest triumphed at the Henley Royal Regatta. In 1928, and again in 1930, the cherished "Diamond Sculls" were won by these Toronto stalwarts. The fame of these young oarsmen aroused enormous public interest, and the Exhibition arranged a series of rowing events which included sculling races for the professional championship of the world.

It was in this era that a young Australian, Bobby Pearce, attracted world attention. As an amateur sculler, Pearce won the singles championship at the 1928 Olympics, a win he repeated two years later at the British Empire Games. In 1931, he won the "Diamond Sculls" and became the first man to hold all three titles.

After taking up residence at Hamilton, Ontario, Pearce came under the tutelage of Walter Obernesser, a former oarsman and a coach of considerable repute. Pearce turned professional in 1933, to row at the Exhibition against the world's champion, Ted Phelps, of England, for a purse of $5,000 to the winner. Pearce, who had never been beaten, was guaranteed $2,500 to win, lose, or draw. The race, over a three mile course, was no contest, as Pearce was an easy winner by one-quarter mile.

This was a performance that Pearce was to repeat regularly at the C.N.E., and, through the remaining years of the decade he had a stranglehold on the professional singles championship of the world. During this time, he defeated such outstanding oarsmen as Eric Phelps, Bert Barry, Jack Beresford, Dick

Southwood, all of England; Bill Miller, of Philadelphia; and the Australians, Evans Paddon, George Cook and Percy See. Of these, Beresford in particular, had enjoyed a sparkling and versatile rowing career. He had won the "Diamond Sculls" on four occasions (1920-1924-1925-1926); was the winner of five Olympic medals — three gold and two silver; and a two-time winner of the world's sculling championship, which he first won in 1924. This was a record unparalleled by few oarsmen.

In 1934, the Exhibition had gathered former oarsmen to officiate at the championship event, and the crowds enjoyed the rare opportunity of mingling with such celebrities as Jake Gaudaur, Lou Scholes, Joe Wright, Jr., Jack Guest, and Joe Wright, Sr.

Amateur rowing was included in the regattas, and all types of races were provided for clubs from Canada and the United States, with special events for boys. On one occasion, the Canadian champion eight-oar crew from the Hamilton Leander Club, settled the inter-city controversy as to which crew was best by gaining a decisive victory over longstanding rivals from the Ottawa and Argonaut clubs.

The one mile Canadian amateur singles sculling championship for the Joe Wright, Sr. Challenge Trophy was instituted in 1937. The event was won by Joe Burk, of Philadelphia, for three consecutive years. Upon his return home, after the third victory, Burk was selected the United States Athlete of the Year.

During the early 1940's, a young Hamiltonian, Jake Gaudaur, won the race for the Joe Wright Trophy in faster time than the record previously set by Burk. His mentor, Bobby Pearce, possibly hoping that Gaudaur might emulate the sculling feats of his famous father, scoffed at the decision to forsake rowing for a career in football. What Jake Gaudaur, Jr. could have accomplished as an oarsman will ever remain a

Bobby Pearce from Hamilton, Ontario was for many years the world's foremost sculler. He's seen with Eric Phelps of England

matter for conjecture, but the phenomenal success that he attained in his chosen sport has earned him lasting fame in Canadian football.

After the War, the Canadian one mile championship was won by John Kelly, Jr., a Philadelphian, and "Diamond Sculls" winner. In 1949, the race attracted only three competitors, and with public, as well as competitive interest, at a low ebb, the event was not re-scheduled at a C.N.E. regatta, and the trophy was withdrawn from competition.

In the previous year, the ladies' ability to row was seen when two eight-oar crews, from the St. Catharines Girls' Rowing Club, demonstrated their art in an exhibition race.

The great public enthusiasm, engendered in earlier years by the prowess of brilliant Toronto oarsmen, had declined. Professional competition at the Fair was a thing of the past, and rowing action at the waterfront centered on amateur events.

With the exception of 1969, rowing was an attraction at the Fair until 1970. During these years, the championships were sanctioned by the Canadian Association of Amateur Oarsmen, and on various occasions, competition was provided by crews from the rowing clubs from Brockville, Hamilton, Buffalo, De-

troit, Lachine, St. Catharines, London, Windsor, and the Argonauts and Dons of Toronto.

Johnny Pearce, of Hamilton, distinguished himself in 1955, by winning the quarter-mile dash as well as the junior and senior singles. Sometime later, in 1961 to be exact, Andy Binda, of Ottawa, won the lightweight singles, which spoiled a clean sweep by St. Catharines' oarsmen, who were victorious in seven of the eight events. At the regatta of 1966, Argonaut crews won six races in the rough waters caused by the swells of speeding powerboats in the 100-mile marathon. The next year, a characterization of the former Governor Simcoe arrived at the rowing championships by longboat. His crew did not display the polish and ability of competing oarsmen. in 1970, evidently much at home in the choppy waters, Argonaut crews triumphed in all eight races for a clean sweep.

After an absence of five years, rowing returned to the Fair in 1975, and keen rivalry resulted in exciting competition. The Hamilton Rowing Club took the heavy-eights events and became the first winners of the George Duthie Memorial Trophy. Argonauts captured three first, two second, and two third placings to gain an overall points total for the eight races.

Toronto Harbour Commission

The Toronto Harbour Commission (THC) and the Canadian National Exhibition (CNE) have a special relationship. One that goes back to the very beginning of the fairgrounds. In fact, right back to a time when the CNE was a little smaller than the 350-acre site that is so familiar to Torontonians of today.

When the THC set out its master plan for waterfront development, the CNE would eventually benefit by the addition of some 200 acres of waterfront lands and the construction of Boulevard Drive, which in the early 1920s served as the new access to the exhibition.

The new roadway was completed to Dowling Avenue in December, 1921. In less than a year the next mile of Lakeshore Boulevard was constructed to connect with the exhibition grounds at the westerly entrance.

The 54-foot wide highway took the place of Lake Shore Road. Immediately upon its completion, streetcar railway tracks were laid which would eventually bring thousands of visitors to the annual exhibition.

A little-known fact about the construction of Boulevard Drive is that the top soil used in the project was actually "imported" from Pickering, Ontario. Since the top soil was a commodity in great demand, the THC purchased a 96-acre farm in Pickering to ensure an adequate supply.

Left Page Top:
Life guards get an early morning tow 1931

Bottom:
Exhausted swimmer is given first aid 1932

A railway siding was built at the farm for "cheap and expeditious handling of the material". Dump trucks then took the loam on the last leg of the journey to the western waterfront. The 'Pickering Connection' provided some 40,000 cubic yards of good top soil used in the construction of Boulevard Drive.

Less than 20 years ago, the THC was still adding to the lands south of the fairgrounds. In 1960 and 1961, when the Gardiner Expressway carved a path through part of the CNE's northern boundary, the Harbour Commission was asked to create some 200 acres of land, through landfill operations, around Lakeshore Boulevard and to the water's edge.

This project brought the CNE to its present size and ended the THC's involvement in the physical expansion of the fairgrounds.

Back in 1930, the harbour commission made another contribution to the exhibition when THC tugs moved the original 184 foot Douglas Fir flagpole from the harbour to the CNE grounds. The tree had been transported to Toronto via the Panama Canal by a Canada Steamships Line vessel.

Over the years the THC's physical presence at the exhibition has also involved the familiar sight of the khaki-uniformed Toronto Harbour Police. The waterborne-unit, which is operated by the THC, for the City of Toronto, has almost become synonymous with the exhibition's marathon swims, air shows and boat races over the last several decades.

The history of the harbour police force goes back even further than the CNE's 100 years. Since the formation of the original Toronto Life Saving and Police Patrol Service, thousands of missions and rescues have been performed on the waterfront, many of them during the hot summer days of the annual exhibition.

In the 20s and 30s, when the Wrigley Marathon swims were in their heyday, the harbour police would patrol the cold waters of Lake Ontario, keeping a close watch on all the contestants. A fleet of lifeguards in small rowboats would actually keep pace with some of the swimmers, while the larger police patrol boats acted as both watchdogs and emergency units, ready to speed to the rescue of an exhausted swimmer or take a contestant out of the lake and administer first aid.

So popular were these swims that bleachers had to be constructed along the CNE waterfront to accommodate the crowds. Of course, those spectators lucky enough to be on board the official boat, steamer Dalhousie City, were right in the middle of the action.

George Ragen, who retired as Superintendent of the harbour police in 1975, still recalls his days as a lifeguard working the marathon swims.

On the starting line of the Telegram Tugboat Race

On a Collision Course

The Wrigley Marathons were always held during the CNE and lifeguards were always on hand to help tired swimmers out of the water and escort others requiring medical attention. Ragen remembers the Wrigley Marathons as one of his tougher assignments.

The grease-covered swimmers were almost impossible to pull out of the water until the lifeguards provided themselves with several short lengths of thick rope which they would put under the swimmers' arms to haul them out.

"That first year as a lifeguard I really got covered in grease, even my clothes which I was carrying in the boat with me,," he said.

"I remember coming home in the early hours one morning, completely tired out, and climbing into the bath to wash off the sticky grease. The next thing I knew, my father was washing me off. I had fallen asleep in the tub."

There were many long, hard hours put in by the harbour police officers and lifeguards in the days of the special aquatic events at the CNE.

In 1921, the Harbour Police were there when during the second heat of the International Displacement Gold Challenge Cup Speed Boat Race, two of the launches crashed in a spectacular accident in front of the grandstand. The driver of the Claire III, which had already crossed the finish line and had won the race, was pulled from the water and rushed to a harbour police boat. The launch sped to the THC's docks but the driver died before reaching the hospital. The wreckage of the other motor boat, the Leopold VI, was towed to a slip at the foot of Spadina. The Claire had sunk immediately upon impact.

In 1932, with water sports more popular than ever at the CNE, the THC completed additional work on the seawall in front of the grounds. The reconstructed seawall, with a promenade for thousands of visitors on the edge of the aquatic course, was turned over to Mayor W. J. Stewart of Toronto, who in turn presented it to President William Inglis of the CNE. The work had been completed just in time for the August opening of the exhibition.

The project included narrowing the channel inside the seawall by some 20 feet. (The filled in land would eventually house a grandstand). Also, cribbing was placed inside the breakwater gaps to ensure smoother water for swimming and boating events. The new aquatic course was ideal for regattas since the newly-created straightaway provided the width and length necessary for keen, unhampered contests.

There were also the exciting Telegram Trophy Races for sailboats, which would have the crowds hanging onto their seats for breathtaking finishes in which the yachts would overtake one another until the last few seconds of the race. The race for the silver cup was celebrating its 10th anniversary in 1932, when harbour police boats escorted the winners to victory.

Lifesavers also had a busy day when the Royal Canadian Yacht Club staged the largest regatta in the CNE's history. More than 250 yachts and dinghies dotted the waters off the seawall during the 1947 exhibition. It was the first of many such events which attracted visitors to the waterfront.

And, who could forget the exciting tug boat races of the early 1960s. The THC's diesel-powered William Rest along with entrants from the Hamilton Harbour Commission, Metro Works Department and private companies put on a spectacular show for the crowds. They plied a two-mile course inside the breakwater leaving a giant wake in their paths. It was an awesome sight as the older steam tugs and high-powered diesels circled the course vying for a trophy.

The Ned Hanlan, which now is permanently berthed on land near the Marine Museum at Exhibition Park, won the honor several years in a row.

The
People
Place—

Officials Who Have Opened
The Canadian National Exhibition

1878 The Earl of Dufferin*
1879 The Marquis of Lorne*
1880 Sir John Beverley Robinson,
Lieutenant Governor of Ontario
1881 Sir John Beverley Robinson,
Lieutenant Governor of Ontario
1882 Hon. Oliver Mowat, Premier of Ontario
1883 The Marquis of Lorne*
1884 Sir John Beverley Robinson,
Lieutenant Governor of Ontario
1885 Sir John Beverley Robinson,
Lieutenant Governor of Ontario
1886 Sir John Beverley Robinson,
Lieutenant Governor of Ontario
1887 Lord Lansdowne*
1888 Lord Stanley of Preston*
1889 Rt. Hon. Sir John A. Macdonald, Prime Minister of Canada
1890 Rt. Hon. Earl of Aberdeen*
1891 Major General Herbert
1892 Sir George A. Kirkpatrick, Lieutenant Governor of Ontario
1893 Sir George A. Kirkpatrick, Lieutenant Governor of Ontario
1894 Rt. Hon. Sir J. S. D. Thompson, Prime Minister of Canada
1895 Sir George A. Kirkpatrick, Lieutenant Governor of Ontario
1896 Hon. Arthur Sturgis, Hardy, Premier of Ontario
1897 Lady Kirkpatrick
1898 Sir Oliver Mowat, Lieutant Governor of Ontario
1899 Major General E. T. H. Hutton, C.B.
1900 Hon. Geo. W. Ross, LL.D., Premier of Ontario
1901 Rt. Hon. Sir Wilfrid Laurier, Prime Minister of Canada
1902 Rt. Hon. Earl Dundonald
1903 Rt. Hon. Lord Strathcona and Mount Royal
1904 Rt. Hon. Mortimer Clark, LL.D.,
Lieutenant Governor of Ontario
1905 Rt. Hon. Earl Grey, G.C., M.C.
1906 Lord Strathcona, Canadian High Commissioner
1907 Sir Wilfrid Laurier, Prime Minister of Canada
1908 Sir Louis Jette, Lieutenant Governor of Quebec
1909 Admiral, Lord Charles Beresford
1910 One Flag — Royal Canadian Navy
1911 Rt. Hon. Earl Gray, G.C., M.C.*
1912 His Royal Highness, the Duke of Connaught*
1913 Hon. R. L. Borden, K.C., Prime Minister of Canada
1914 Sir James Whitney, Premier of Ontario
1915 Hon. Lieut.-Col. J. S. Hendrie, C.V.O.,
Lieutenant Governor of Ontario
1916 Hon. Sir George Halfey Perley, K.M.-M.G., B.A.,
High Commissioner for Canada in London, England
1917 His Excellency, the Duke of Devonshire, K.C., G.C.V.O.*
1918 Lord Shaughnessy, President, Canadian Pacific Railway
1919 His Royal Highness, the Prince of Wales
1920 Sir Auckland Geddes, British Ambassador to Washington
1921 Baron Byng*
1922 Hon. Henry Cockshutt, Lieutenant Governor of Ontario
1923 Prof. F. G. Banting, Discoverer of Insulin
1924 Admiral Field, Commander, North Atlantic Squadron
1925 Hon. G. Howard Ferguson, Premier of Ontario
1926 Sir T. Vijayaraghavacharya, Indian Potentate
1927 Rt. Hon. Wm. Lyon Mackenzie King,
Prime Minister of Canada
1928 His Excellency, Right Hon. Viscount Willingdon*
1929 Hon. William Donald Ross, LL.D.,
Lieutenant Governor of Ontario
1930 E. W. Beatty, Esq., K.C.,
President, Canadian Pacific Railway
1931 Admiral of the Fleet, Lord Jellicoe

1932 Rt. Hon. R. B. Bennett, K.C., Prime Minister of Canada
1933 The Hon. Geo. S. Henry, Premier of Ontario
1934 The Earl of Bessborough*
1935 Colonel, The Hon. Herbert A. Bruce,
Lieutenant Governor of Ontario
1936 Hon. Mitchell F. Hepburn, Premier of Ontario
1937 Hon. Newton W. Rowell, Chief Justice of Ontario
1938 Lord Stanley, Secretary of State for Dominion Affairs
1939 Lord Maugham, Lord High Chancellor of Britain
1940 Rt. Hon. Earl of Athlone*
1941 His Royal Highness, the Duke of Kent
1947 Rt. Hon. William Lyon Mackenzie King,
Prime Minister of Canada
1948 Rear Admiral the Earl Mountbatten of Burma, K.G.
1949 Field Marshall the Right Honourable Viscount Alexander of
Tunis, K.G., G.C.B., G.C.M.G., C.S.I., D.S.O., M.C.,
LL.D.*
1950 The Right Hon. C. D. Howe, P.C.,
Minister of Trade and Commerce
1951 The Hon. George C. Marshall, Secretary of Defence, U.S.A.
1952 Rt. Hon. Vincent Massey, P.C., C.H.*
First Native-born Governor-General
1953 Field Marshall the Right Honourable the Viscount
Montgomery of Alametin, K.G., G.C.B., D.S.O., Deputy
Supreme Commander the Allied Powers in Europe
1954 Her Royal Highness, The Duchess of Kent,
C.I., G.C.-V.O., G.B.E.
1955 Lord Rowallan, K.B.E., M.C., T.D., LL.D.
1956 The Hon. Lester B. Pearson,
Secretary of State for External Affairs
1957 The Hon. L. O. Breithaupt, Lieutenant Governor of Ontario
1958 Rt. Hon. John G. Diefenbaker, Prime Minister of Canada
1959 The Admiral of the Fleet, The Earl Mountbatten of Burma,
K.G., P.C., G.C.B., G.C.S.L., G.C.I.B., G.C.V.O., D.S.O.,
Chief of the United Kingdon Defence Staff
1960 Hon. J. Keiller Mackay, D.S.O., V.D., Q.C., LL.D.,
Lieutenant Governor of Ontario
1961 Hon. Leslie M. Frost, Q.C., LL.D., D.C.L.,
Premier of Ontario
1962 Hon. Jean Lesage, Prime Minister of Quebec
1963 Most Reverend Dr. Arthur Michael Ramsey
1964 The Hon. W. Earl Rowe, P.C.(C.), LL.D.,
Lieutenant Governor of Ontario
1965 The Right Hon. Lester B. Pearson,
Prime Minister of Canada
1966 Lord Thomson of Fleet
1967 The Rt. Hon. Vincent Massey, C.C., C.H.*
1968 The Hon. John P. Robarts, P.C., Q.C., Premier of Ontario
1969 The Rt. Hon. Pierre Elliott Trudeau, P.C., M.P.,
Prime Minister of Canada
1970 Her Royal Highness Princess Margriet of the Netherlands
1971 His Grace the Duke of Argyle, T.D., Mac Calein Mor
1972 His Excellency, The Rt. Hon. Rolland Michener, CC, C.D.*
1973 William Leonard Higgitt, Commissioner,
Royal Canadian Mounted Police
1974 The Hon. William G. Davis, Q.C., Premier of Ontario
1975 Gordon Sinclair, Broadcaster and Entertainer
1976 Bob Hope, C.B.E.
1977 Hon. Pauline M. McGibbon, O.C., B.A., LL.D., D.U. (Ott.),
B.A.A. (Theatre), Lieutenant Governor of Ontario
1978 His Excellency, The Right Honourable Jules Leger,
C.C., C.M.M., C.D., Governor General of Canada*

---

*denotes Governor General of Canada

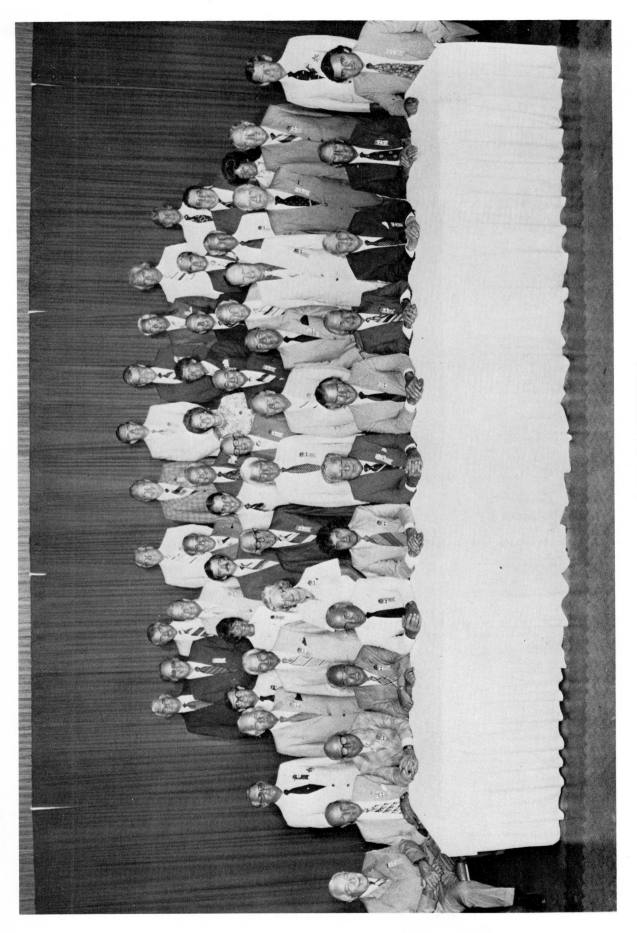

1978 BOARD OF DIRECTORS